THE LAST
ACTOR-MANAGERS

1 Sir Johnston
   Forbes-Robertson
2 Sir Herbert Tree
3 Sir George
   Alexander
4 Sir Frank Benson
5 Lewis Waller
6 Sir John Martin-
   Harvey
7 H. B. Irving
8 Laurence Irving
9 Oscar Asche
10 Harley
   Granville-Barker

THE LAST
ACTOR-MANAGERS

by

HESKETH PEARSON

With Illustrations from
the Raymond Mander and Joe Mitchenson Theatre Collection

Biography Index Reprint Series

 BOOKS FOR LIBRARIES PRESS
FREEPORT, NEW YORK

PN2597
P4

TO

MY FRIEND

WALTER HAVERS

INTERNATIONAL STANDARD BOOK NUMBER:
0-8369-8072-7

LIBRARY OF CONGRESS CATALOG CARD NUMBER:
77-148225

PRINTED IN THE UNITED STATES OF AMERICA

INTRODUCTION

FOR some two hundred years, from the time of Thomas Betterton at the end of the seventeenth century to the time of Beerbohm Tree at the beginning of the twentieth, the London stage was dominated by a succession of famous actors whose popularity enabled them to dictate the policy of their theatres and who eventually became known as actor-managers. Most of them won their reputations by playing the great Shakespearean characters; and though they often adapted the plays or produced emasculated versions in order to make the plots or their own parts, as they thought, more effective, it was entirely due to them that Shakespeare, or mangled Shakespeare, held the stage from the reign of Charles II to the reign of George V. The war of 1914–18 practically brought their supremacy to a close, though some of them managed to keep going for a few years after it was over.

Strangely enough, their popularity was at its height just before they disappeared from the scene; and when I arrived in London in 1906 most of the leading theatres were run by them, each theatre had a policy of presenting plays that fitted the personality or suited the taste of its director, and there were no signs that the actor-manager system had entered the last decade of its existence. Light comedy was provided by Sir Charles Wyndham, the most accomplished actor of 'modern' parts I have ever seen, by Sir John Hare, who gave lifelike impersonations of eccentrics, by Cyril Maude, whose performances of old men were unapproached, and by Charles Hawtrey, who could make a commonplace remark sound witty. Omitting the names of those whose careers are considered

v

in the following pages, there were also Arthur Bourchier, who usually produced serious modern dramas but whose best performance was as Henry VIII in Tree's production of that play; Fred Terry, who could have been the best Falstaff of his age but who preferred to enjoy leisure on the handsome profits of such popular melodramas as *The Scarlet Pimpernel* and *Sweet Nell of Old Drury*; Matheson Lang, a sound romantic actor; and Gerald Du Maurier, who wasted his gifts on sensational or sentimental pieces. Wyndham, Hare and the Kendals, were the contemporaries of Sir Henry Irving, and their more notable managerial enterprises occurred long before I saw them act. But the reason I have not dealt with Maude, Hawtrey, Bourchier, Terry, Lang and Du Maurier, is that their productions did not appeal to me, Cyril Maude's revivals of the Old Comedies having taken place before my time.

In 1911 I went on the stage and in the course of the next few years met all the managers included in this volume and several of those mentioned above, having already seen most of them in their famous parts. It seems to me that the theatre has suffered by the disappearance of their class, that their merits outweighed their deficiencies, that even when their taste was bad it was more satisfactory than the later alternative of running a theatre with no taste at all, and that in art the daring of an individual is preferable to the discretion of a committee.

CONTENTS

ILLUSTRATIONS

Frontispiece

Sir Johnston Forbes-Robertson; Sir Herbert Tree; Sir George Alexander; Sir Frank Benson; Lewis Waller; Sir John Martin-Harvey; H. B. Irving; Laurence Irving; Oscar Asche; Harley Granville-Barker

viii

ILLUSTRATIONS

ix

Waller and Madge Titheradge in *Bardelys the Magnificent*
—— and Grace Lane in *Miss Elizabeth's Prisoner*
—— and Evelyn Millard in *The Harlequin King*
—— and Evelyn Millard as Brutus and Portia in Tree's production of *Julius Caesar* (1898)
—— and Evelyn Millard as Othello and Desdemona
—— as Henry V
—— and Evelyn Millard as Romeo and Juliet

Between pages 48 and 49

Sir John Martin-Harvey as Richard III*
—— as Sir Dagonet in Henry Irving's production of *King Arthur* (1895)
—— and N. de Silva as Hamlet and Ophelia
Scene from Reinhardt's production at Covent Garden of *Oedipus Rex*, with Martin-Harvey in the name-part*
Martin-Harvey and N. de Silva in *The Breed of the Treshams*
—— as Sydney Carton in *The Only Way*
Scene from Martin-Harvey's production of *The Breed of the Treshams*

Between pages 50 and 51

Martin-Harvey in *The Corsican Brothers*
—— in *A Cigarette Maker's Romance*
—— as Boy O'Carroll
—— as Pelléas
H. B. Irving in *The Bells*
—— as Charles I
—— as Markheim
—— and Lewis Waller as Othello and Iago
—— and Dorothea Baird in *Louis XI*
—— as Hyde, and Eille Norwood, in *Dr Jekyll and Mr Hyde*
—— and Irene Vanbrugh in *The Admirable Crichton*
—— as Wogan in *Princess Clementina*
Scene from H. B. Irving's production of *The Lyons Mail*

Between pages 62 and 63

Laurence Irving and Mabel Hackney in *The Unwritten Law*
Scene from Laurence Irving's production of *The Lily*
Laurence Irving and Mabel Hackney in *Typhoon*
Oscar Asche as Falstaff, and Roy Royston as Robin, in *The Merry Wives of Windsor*
Scene from Asche's production of *The Merry Wives of Windsor*
Asche as Chu-Chin-Chow*
—— as Christopher Sly in *The Taming of the Shrew*
—— as Petruchio in *The Taming of the Shrew*
—— and Lily Brayton in *Kismet*

ILLUSTRATIONS

Between pages 70 and 71

Scene from Asche's production of *Mameena*
Asche and Lily Brayton in *Count Hannibal*
—— and Lily Brayton in *Measure for Measure*
—— as Bottom in his production of *A Midsummer Night's Dream*

Between pages 74 and 75

Harley Granville-Barker and Bernard Shaw (*c.* 1900)
Ellen Terry and Fred Kerr in *Captain Brassbound's Conversion*
Granville-Barker, Fanny Brough, and Charles Goodhart in *Mrs Warren's Profession* (1902)
The Forum Scene in Tree's production of *Julius Caesar*: Coronation Gala Performance at His Majesty's Theatre, 1911
Scene from Granville-Barker's production of *Androcles and the Lion* (1913): Ben Webster as the Captain; Lillah McCarthy as Lavinia; Baliol Holloway as the Menagerie Keeper; Leon Quartermaine as the Emperor; Edward Sillward as the Lion; O. P. Heggie as Androcles; Alfred Brydone as Ferrovius; Herbert Hewetson as the Editor
Scene from Granville-Barker's production of *The Winter's Tale* (1912). Stanley Drewitt as Camillo; Cathleen Nesbitt as Perdita; H. O. Nicholson as the Old Shepherd; Dennis Neilson-Terry as Florizel

Between pages 78 and 79

Scene from Granville-Barker's production of *Twelfth Night* (1912) with Henry Ainley as Malvolio; Hayden Coffin as Feste; Evelyn Millard as Olivia
Scene from Granville-Barker's production of *A Midsummer Night's Dream* (1914)
The Death Scene from *The Doctor's Dilemma* (1906). Trevor Lowe as Reporter; James Hearn as Cutler Walpole; Ben Webster as Sir Colenso Ridgeon; Lillah McCarthy as Jennifer; Granville-Barker as Dubedat; William Farren, Jr., as Sir Patrick Cullen; Eric Lewis as Sir Ralph Bloomfield Bonnington
Louis Calvert as Undershaft and Granville-Barker as Cusins in *Major Barbara* (1905)

Photos marked * are by *Daily Mirror*

xi

'It is my considered opinion that there is far less imposture and make-believe in the fine arts than in the so-called serious professions. Reading this life of yours I perceive that as compared with our Lord Chief Justices, our front bench politicians, our medical baronets, our archbishops, you, the actor, stand out with extraordinary distinction and loveableness because you are not a humbug. Instead of being the man who pretended to be Hamlet, you are precisely the man who never pretended to be anybody but Forbes-Robertson playing Hamlet. Beside the judge in his ermine and scarlet pretending to be justice, and the fashionable doctor pretending to be the Omniscient master of life and death, and the priest with his apostolic succession and his bunch of the keys of heaven and hell, you, whether as actor or painter, have the advantage of a celebrity that is not idolatry and a regard that is untainted by a secret abhorrence of the angry ape posing as a god.'

(From a letter by Bernard Shaw to Sir Johnston Forbes-Robertson on the publication of his autobiography *A Player under Three Reigns*, 1925.)

SIR JOHNSTON FORBES-ROBERTSON
(1853–1937)

IT is an odd fact that the only famous actor I have ever seen who was incapable of giving an indifferent performance of any conceivable part was the only famous actor I have ever known who did not like acting. Forbes-Robertson used to say that he would rather be a painter than anything else in the world. Asked why he went on the stage, he replied, 'Six guineas a week, from Phelps.' Yet he had been blessed with every possible quality for success as an actor: classical features, an engaging manner, a natural elegance of speech and movement, and a rich melodious voice with the tone of an organ. If he had played Charley's Aunt, it would have been a distinguished bit of work. As it was, he played Hamlet so perfectly that he made other actors in the part seem pretentious, affected, dull and commonplace by comparison. I have seen some thirty Hamlets, including the 'stars' in every London revival of the play between 1905 and 1950, but Robertson's was so far superior to all the others that there was no second-best: there was simply Forbes-Robertson—and the rest. The general public seemed to agree, because I fancy he was the only actor in stage-history who could claim that he had made more money out of *Hamlet* than from any other of his productions. Actors with not half his skill had big moments in their performances the like of which he never knew. What made his Hamlet unique was not his impressive handling of this or that particular scene, but that from first to last it was perfectly natural, nobly well-bred, ideally graceful, flawlessly spoken, and so charming that one could see it again and again, and twice in a day, yet never tire of it. He and Ellen

Terry were the only two players in my experience who delivered the language of Shakespeare as if it were their natural idiom and whose beauty of diction matched the beauty of the words. But he did not enjoy doing it for a living, and after he had acted Hamlet for the last time in his sixty-fourth year he confessed that he removed his costume 'with no sort of regret, but rather with a great sense of relief'. Macready had felt the same. He could not bear the sight of a poster with his name on it.

Forbes-Robertson began life studying for the profession of his choice; entered Heatherley's School of Art at the age of sixteen; and became a student at the Royal Academy a year later. But as the eldest of a large family he felt that he ought to earn a living, and though he had no desire to become an actor he followed the advice of friends and went on the stage at the age of twenty. He was very fortunate because quite early in his career the famous Shakespearean player Samuel Phelps took a fancy to him, engaged him, and coached him in all his parts. In this way he learnt the technique that had been handed down from Garrick, through Mrs Siddons and Macready, to Phelps, whose influence and teaching, Robertson affirmed, were mainly responsible for his own achievements. 'I may boast of a good histrionic pedigree', he said. 'There is the good old school and the bad old school and the former is the best school for any time.' As he was the most natural actor of his age, there is obviously something to be said for the good old school.

Though he had learnt his job with Phelps, he probably owed the parts for which he was soon cast to his personal appearance, because he quickly became a leading juvenile. While still in his twenties he played Romeo to the Juliet of the famous Polish actress Modjeska; then he was engaged by the Bancrofts; and before he was thirty Irving gave him the

Forbes-Robertson as Hamlet (1897)

Forbes-Robertson and Gertrude Elliott as Caesar and Cleopatra
in Bernard Shaw's play

Forbes-Robertson
and Gertrude Elliott
in *The Light that Failed*
by Rudyard Kipling

Forbes-Robertson and
Mrs. Patrick Campbell
in *Romeo and Juliet*

Forbes-Robertson as Lancelot
in Henry Irving's production
of *King Arthur*

Forbes-Robertson and Gertrude Elliot
as Shylock and Portia
in *The Merchant of Venice*

Forbes-Robertson and Gertrude Elliott
in *The Passing of the Third Floor Back*

part of Claudio in *Much Ado About Nothing* at the Lyceum Theatre. There followed a tour of America as Mary Anderson's leading man, and an appearance as Leontes in her production of *The Winter's Tale* at the Lyceum in London, for which he designed the dresses. Then came six years with John Hare, and another engagement with Irving to play Buckingham in *Henry VIII*. All this time, as he was never out of a job, he could go on with his painting.

Henry Irving used to tour the provinces or America every autumn, so Forbes-Robertson took the Lyceum Theatre for three seasons during the chief's absence, and, with Mrs Patrick Campbell as his leading lady, produced, among other plays, *Romeo and Juliet*, *Macbeth*, *The School for Scandal*, and *Hamlet*, the last of which was financially backed by Horatio Bottomley. It was in September 1897, when Forbes-Robertson was forty-four years old, that he first played Hamlet, which inspired Bernard Shaw to write a great appraisal of it in *The Saturday Review* and to conceive a historical play, *Caesar and Cleopatra*, with magnificent parts for Robertson and Mrs Patrick Campbell. But Mrs Campbell made fun of it, and years elapsed before that remarkable work was seen on the stage. Meanwhile Robertson wanted to give Shaw's melodrama *The Devil's Disciple* a full dress production at the Comedy Theatre, London. Shaw objected that it was too late in the season. Robertson asked: was that final? Shaw replied that it was. Robertson looked him straight in the face, turned and took Mrs Shaw in his arms, kissed her, and stalked out of the room. But he played it in the provinces during 1900, and married his leading lady, Gertrude Elliott, who thereafter gave him invaluable support in all his productions, two of his biggest successes shortly following their marriage: *Mice and Men* and *The Light that Failed*, the last being a dramatic version of Kipling's story, in which Robertson gave

3

an almost unbearably pathetic impersonation of the painter-hero. Both these were produced at the Lyric Theatre in London. *Othello* and *The Merchant of Venice* were duly added to their repertory; and although Robertson could portray neither the violence of the Moor nor the virulence of the Jew, anyone who loved the plays primarily for the music of their poetry would rather have heard him read them than have seen the finest cast of actors perform them, so beautifully did he deliver the speeches.

But apart from his performance of Hamlet, Forbes-Robertson's most distinguished contribution to the theatre of his time was Shaw's *Caesar and Cleopatra*. It was in fact his most important contribution, because he was quite as much the 'only begetter' of Shaw's Caesar as Richard Burbage had been of Shakespeare's Hamlet. Without him Shaw would not have written the play. At first he dared not risk such a heavy production, and seven years passed before the opportunity occurred of putting it on for a run in New York. Shaw rehearsed the company in England, and Forbes-Robertson assured me that he was a heaven-sent producer, but added, rather unexpectedly: 'Poor old darling!'

Having put the company through their paces, Shaw told Robertson that 'the rehearsals have convinced me that I did this job extraordinarily well for you. . . . When Hamlets are down to six a penny, there will still be only one Caesar.' The play was produced in the autumn of 1906 and was far more intelligently received by the American critics than it was a year later by the English ones. Shaw guessed that the London press would fail to do it justice and that the audiences would be puzzled. 'I have no doubt that your Caesar will be a stroke of work that this generation of Londoners has seen nothing of', he told Robertson, adding that the unique merits of his performance would be recognised in time. The London production was at the Savoy Theatre in November 1907, and ran for four weeks. Everything happened exactly as Shaw had foreseen: the critics were silly, the audiences scant. 'Still, it was worth doing', wrote the author to Robertson. 'It put everybody else behind you—restored the perspective of the stage, with the character actor in his place in the middle distance, and the classic actor sunlike above the horizon.' Shaw's second prophecy was also fulfilled, because each visit to a provincial town resulted in larger audiences, and when in 1913 Forbes-Robertson gave a Farewell Season at Drury Lane Theatre *Caesar and Cleopatra* packed the house. Shaw wanted to dramatise a story by Cunninghame Graham about Mahomet, with Robertson in the part of the prophet; but the censor would not have passed it, and moreover Shaw was warned that he would probably be murdered by a Moslem fanatic.

Incidentally Robertson was nearly killed by a careless carpenter during a rehearsal of *Caesar and Cleopatra* on the stage of a Liverpool theatre. I heard of the episode from his assistant stage-manager, Hubert Hine. In the middle of one of Caesar's speeches a hammer fell from the grid missing Robertson by inches. He merely paused for a second, looked up, said quietly 'Please don't do that again'; and continued his speech.

I saw *Caesar and Cleopatra* three times during that month's run at the Savoy, and I cannot remember enjoying any piece of acting so much as Robertson's Caesar. There has been nothing to compare with it on the stage of my time: a great classical actor interpreting to perfection a self-inspired classical part. There may have been passages in his Hamlet that were not rendered as effectively as similar passages in the performances of other actors, though no one can have been so completely satisfying in the part; but there was not a move-ment or an inflection in his Caesar that could have been bettered; and if the play had to wait for another artist to perform the leading character so superbly as Forbes-Robertson, it would never again be seen on the stage. I ought to add that the acting of Cleopatra by his wife, Gertrude Elliott, was worthy of his Caesar.

In September 1908 Forbes-Robertson produced Jerome K. Jerome's play *The Passing of the Third Floor Back* at the St James's Theatre; and it became his chief box-office success. Carlyle would have described it as 'bottled moonshine', and perhaps it is unnecessary to add that no one but Robertson could have made it seem solid. It was the sort of thing that unites the clergy of all denominations. Praises of it were chanted in churches and chapels throughout Great Britain and America, and the dramatic critics joined their voices to the chorus of alleluias. The plot is simple. A Christ-like personage takes a room in a third-rate Bloomsbury boarding-house, comes into contact with its vicious but entertaining inmates, irons out their characters in the course of the play, and leaves them virtuous but tedious. It was exactly what one would expect from a professional humourist in his solemn moments, and those of us who had fully appreciated *Caesar and Cleopatra* were content to leave Jerome's effort to the clergy and the critics.

Robertson himself became weary of the play and sick of his part in it. Hubert Hine sent me the following reminiscence: 'I remember one night standing beside him just before he made his first entrance as "The Stranger" when he suddenly turned his eyes towards heaven and ejaculated "Chr-r-rist! Will they never let me give up this *bloody* part?" A moment later the door of the set opened to show him standing there like a saint, or greater.'

Having played Hamlet at intervals for some twenty years, Forbes-Robertson made his last stage appearance in the part at Harvard University in 1916; and when I begged him four years later to revive the play once more he replied that he could not do so for two reasons—'the main one being that having taken an official farewell, I cannot with any sort of good grace reappear on the stage. The other is that age creeps on me and I doubt if I should have the strength to go through the ordeal of playing so exacting a part. No, I must now leave Hamlet to the younger men.' When he retired I felt that Shakespeare's words had never been so applicable:

> As in a theatre, the eyes of men,
> After a well-graced actor leaves the stage,
> Are idly bent on him that enters next,
> Thinking his prattle to be tedious . . .

On the death of Sir Henry Irving nearly every actor considered that Forbes-Robertson was, by achievement and personal distinction, his rightful successor as head of the profession. In the public mind Beerbohm Tree occupied that position; but their fellow-artists always recognised the pre-eminent qualification of Robertson, who, by the way, was responsible for Irving's burial in Westminster Abbey. There is no reason now why it should not be disclosed that Robertson first got his brother Norman Forbes to ask the Dean of St Paul's Cathedral whether Irving might be buried there. The Dean was very haughty and abruptly refused his permission, adding 'I shall be buried here, you know.' After that the Dean of Westminster was approached; but he insisted that the appeal should be backed by two distinguished members of each leading profession. Pre-paid wires were promptly despatched to all sorts of eminent folk, only two of whom refused their support.

Apart from the courtliness of his manners and the saintliness of his features, Forbes-Robertson had little in common

SIR HEREBRT TREE
(1853–1917)

KNOWN during the greater part of his life as Beerbohm Tree, he liked to be called Sir Herbert Tree after he was knighted; but somehow the Beerbohm has stuck, partly perhaps because he was Max Beerbohm's half-brother. He came at the end of a famous line of actors whose Shakespearean productions or performances earned them a peculiar prestige on the London stage of their time, such as David Garrick, John Philip Kemble, Edmund Kean, William Macready, Samuel Phelps, Henry Irving, and Forbes-Robertson. Yet, although his revivals of Shakespeare's plays gave his management its distinction and placed him in the general estimation at the head of his profession after the death of Irving, it cannot be said that Tree was a great Shakespearean actor. He had an odd personality, quite unfitted to heroic parts, a curious throaty delivery which prevented him from speaking blank verse naturally, and rather bizarre gestures, more in tune with burlesque than with poetry. His Hamlet was accurately described by W. S. Gilbert as funny without being vulgar; his Macbeth could never have fought a battle; his Othello could never have known jealousy, and did not always know Shakespeare's lines; his Antony was anything but an orator in *Julius Caesar* and anything but a lover with Cleopatra; and although his Shylock could be as impressive as his Wolsey was dignified, neither had the authentic Shakespearean ring. Even his humorous impersonations were not in the least like the original characters: his Malvolio was simply himself being very amusing; his Benedick was also himself but not being at

9

all amusing; and though his Falstaff in *The Merry Wives of Windsor* was a rollicking affair, Shaw was right when he said that Tree only wanted one thing to make him an excellent Falstaff in *Henry IV*, Part I, and that was to get born over again as unlike himself as possible.

His productions, however, were the major theatrical events of their period. They were done with the utmost splendour and realism. The wood near Athens in *A Midsummer Night's Dream* had rabbits running about in it; Olivia's Garden in *Twelfth Night* was carpeted with grass and filled with flowers and statuary; the opening scene of *The Tempest* showed a complete ship rocking in a sea the waves of which splashed over the deck and made many in the audience feel squeamish; the rustic scene in *The Winter's Tale* contained a real cottage, a real stream and waterfall, a willow-tree, reeds, and such-like riparian devices; *King John* contained a still-life picture which exercised the ability of the entire company to keep still and look like a picture but did not forward Shakespeare's dramatic intent; in *Richard II* Tree rode through London on horseback, though Shakespeare was content with making another character mention the episode; while the return of Antony to Alexandria, described by Octavius Caesar in a short speech, was presented by Tree as a magnificent tableau, with surging crowds and processions of priests and military marches and the strewing of flowers and the clashing of cymbals and the dances of women and a general conglomeration of sound and colour. He was constantly criticised for the lavishness of his productions, and he once remarked to me 'Shakespearean scholars say I'm wrong in tempting people to come to the theatre and giving them a spectacle instead of Shakespeare. But I prefer a spectacle on the stage to spectacles in the audience.'

Shakespeare might have objected to the sacrifice of his

10

poetry for scenery; but Stephen Phillips, nowadays a much-underrated poet, wrote four of his plays for Tree—*Herod*, *Ulysses*, *Nero* and *Faust*—and allowed for all the pageantry imaginable. The profusion on the stage matched the grandiloquence of the verse, and there never was such a theatrical spectacle as *Nero*, which included the triumphant entry of the emperor into Rome—Tree driving in a chariot drawn by two milk-white steeds with distinguished stage careers—and the burning of the city, when houses crumpled, temples crashed, arches swayed, and flames shot up, the whole being realistic enough to make the more nervous among the audience look for the exit doors or rise from their seats. When Louis Parker's *Joseph and His Brethren* appeared at His Majesty's Theatre, the street outside the stage-door was nightly crammed with camels, oxen, sheep, asses, goats, and the other fauna of Palestine. Their presence in the play largely helped to cram the theatre too. But Tree had just as keen an eye for small details as for big effects. For example, in order to complete the sense of domesticity in a certain scene, he wanted a canary in a cage, which was duly produced for his inspection. But he pointed out that canaries were after all natural, and that the floor of the cage should not be so clean as to suggest that this particular bird was stuffed. At the next rehearsal the stage-manager, too much accustomed to large-scale realism, exhibited the cage. Tree gazed at the floor, and then said: 'Yes . . . yes . . . But this is a canary, not a parrot.' I am aware that this story has been told of Henry Irving, and Mr Percy Nash, who stage-managed for both Irving and Tree, informed me that Irving made the remark to Hawes Craven at the final rehearsal of *The Medicine Man*; but I had it from one of Tree's stage-managers, and it seems more characteristic of him than of Irving.

Like David Garrick, Sir Henry Irving, Sir George

Alexander, Lewis Waller, and many other actors of distinction, Tree started life in business. His father, Julius Beerbohm, was a grain merchant, and the boy worked in his father's city office. But he was a born mimic, and being seized with a desire to act he took the name of Tree and went on the stage. He soon made a reputation in parts of a farcical and macabre nature, and within ten years of his first appearance, when thirty-four years old, he was managing the Haymarket Theatre, where he remained from 1887 till 1897, winning fame as a 'character' actor. Apart from three of Shakespeare's, the only plays he produced which have much interest for us today were Oscar Wilde's second comedy, *A Woman of No Importance*, and Ibsen's *An Enemy of the People*. He had an unqualified admiration for Wilde both as man and playwright, and told me that Wilde could get the better of anyone by his wit, and charm everyone by his manner. He had an answer for everything, said Tree, giving me the following specimen. A stolen letter from Wilde to Lord Alfred Douglas had been sent to Tree, who handed it to Wilde with the remark that the sentiments expressed in it were open to misconstruction. Wilde explained that it was a prose poem, and if put into verse might be printed in such a respectable anthology as the *Golden Treasury*. 'Yes, but it is not in verse', objected Tree. 'That no doubt is why it is not in the *Golden Treasury*', answered Wilde.

Tree's biggest money-maker at the Haymarket was *Trilby*, which never failed to draw good houses whenever it was revived. After its production he built Her Majesty's Theatre just opposite, renaming it His Majesty's on the accession of Edward VII. This he managed from 1897 till his death in 1917, and here he gave his elaborate productions of sixteen of Shakespeare's plays, in which great attention was paid to the commotions of Nature. To take an example: just before his

entrance in *Macbeth* there was a long roll of thunder, a roar
of wind and a rattle of hail; the darkness was suddenly
pierced by blinding flashes of lightning, in which one could
see rocks falling and a stout oak-tree, rent to the roots,
toppling to the earth; following this the elements howled
invisibly for a space; then came an ear-splitting peal of
thunder, a final shriek of the blast, and against the dazzling
background of a lightning-riven sky stood the figure of
Macbeth. Then Shakespeare got a look-in. Emerging from
the theatre after one of these stage-quaking exhibitions into a
real thunderstorm, one had to admit that Nature put up a
pretty feeble imitation of what several barrels of stones and
a few sheets of tin could do in His Majesty's.

It was during a rehearsal of *Macbeth* that I noticed the
grave difficulties which a producer who is also a 'star' actor
has to face. Tree was so much concerned with his own performance that nothing else seemed to matter. At one point,
when Macbeth describes how he finds the dead King Duncan,
he has to say:

> there, the murderers,
> Steep'd in the colours of their trade, their daggers
> Unmannerly breech'd with gore—

at which Tree broke off to complain 'They won't be able to
see me from that box. Will that gentleman oblige me by
moving out of the way? Thank you.'

Bernard Shaw realised during the production of *Pygmalion*
at His Majesty's (1914) that Tree's sole concern was to
liven up his part, not having noticed that the author had
already done so, and that he was leaving everything else to
chance. Shaw therefore attended to everything else, so
thoroughly indeed that one day Tree was gently sarcastic. 'I
seem to have heard or read somewhere', he said, 'that plays

have actually been produced, and performances given, in this theatre, under its present management, before you came. According to you, that couldn't have happened. How do you account for it?' 'I can't account for it', Shaw replied. 'I suppose you put a notice in the papers that a performance will take place at half-past eight, and take the money at the doors. Then you *have* to do the play somehow. There is no other way of accounting for it.' In fact Tree entirely depended on the experience of his actors and the efficiency of his managers, especially his stage-manager Cecil King, to get the job done, and rehearsals were sometimes as chaotic as they were invariably exhausting. He seldom interfered with his cast, unless they got between him and a box, and such advice as he gave was not always helpful. I heard him once say to an actor: 'I want you to suggest—well, you know, don't you?'— he made vague gestures in the air, and then added 'A cross between a whitebait and a marmoset.' Tree was no judge of plays, choosing them mostly because they provided him with showy parts. He turned down Barrie's *Peter Pan*, which became a fabulous success, merely because he did not care for the part of Captain Hook, in which by the way he would have been excellent. When I asked him why he had rejected it, he replied mysteriously 'God knows, and I have promised to tell no one else.'

Apart from Shakespeare, Shaw's *Pygmalion*, the plays of Stephen Phillips, and an all-'star' revival of Sheridan's *The School for Scandal*, Tree's management of His Majesty's Theatre was mainly notable for his vividly represented 'character' parts, sometimes comic, sometimes sinister, always rather bizarre, and his versions of *David Copperfield*, in which, unexpectedly, he was more moving as Peggotty than amusing as Micawber, and *Oliver Twist*, in which he played Fagin, a character that suited his fantastic style to perfection. But the

A MASTER OF MAKE-UP

Tree as Fagin
in *Oliver Twist*

Tree as Shylock
in *The Merchant of Venice*

Tree as Paragot
in *The Beloved Vagabond*

Tree as Svengali
in *Trilby*

Tree as Ulysses
in Stephen Phillips's play

Tree as D'Artagnan
in *The Three Musketeers*

Tree as Macbeth

Tree as Richard II

Tree as the High Priest in *False Gods* by Brieux

Tableau—Magna Charta—in Tree's production of *King John*

Tree, Arthur Bourchier, and Violet Vanbrugh
as Wolsey, the King, and Katharine, in *Henry VIII*

Drunken Scene from Tree's production of *Antony and Cleopatra*
with Lyn Harding as Enobarbus (left) ; Tree as Antony (leaning down) ;
Norman Forbes as Lepidus (lying down) ; Basil Gill as Octavius (looking u[

line that got the biggest laugh in *Oliver Twist* was not by Dickens. It was a 'gag' by Tree. When he heard Mr Brownlow refer to Fagin as 'an old Jew', he turned to his companion and said 'D'ye 'ear that? 'E called me a Jew', which brought down the house.

Tree's best performances however were not always in such gruesome parts as Fagin and Svengali. As Thackeray's Colonel Newcome he could be very restrained and pathetic; as Paragot in *The Beloved Vagabond* he was delightful; and as Beethoven he was able to blind one to the badness of the play. His genius for getting into the skin of a part, physically and mentally, was never better exemplified than in *Beethoven*. Louis Parker, who had adapted the play from the French, said that when Tree first appeared at the dress-rehearsal the entire company gasped with surprise. There entered 'a short stocky, square-set little man, with dark eyes. His head was Beethoven's head.' Tree was tall, lanky, blue-eyed, the very opposite to Beethoven in build and features; and I, too, experienced a shock when I found myself next to him at Covent Garden, where he was giving an act of the play at a charity matinée, because, though expecting his appearance, I completely failed to recognise him and was under the strong impression of looking down at a man whose eyes were normally on a level with my own. These metamorphoses were uncanny, and what made His Majesty's the most thrilling theatre in the world was that even when he was hopelessly miscast Tree's acting was so clever, so inventive, so varied, so intensely interesting, that for unalloyed entertainment one would rather see him in a bad play than anyone else in a good one. His range as an actor was amazing. The funniest piece of work I have ever seen on the stage was his burglar-lunatic in *The Van Dyck*, a bit of pure foolery, while in many respects the most moving Shakespearean performance I can recall was his Richard II. But this is not to say that his Richard, or any of his characters, was always, or often, well done. He quickly got bored with a part and would 'walk through' it, thinking of something else. I have seen him act greatly and outrageously in the same play within the same week; and when he described one of his productions as 'an obstinate success' he really meant that it was getting on his nerves.

One often wondered how His Majesty's was kept going at all, because Tree always seemed to be up in the clouds and never counted the cost of anything. I remember sitting in his dressing-room one evening when his business-manager Henry Dana was trying to explain the figures in a ledger. Tree listlessly turned the pages over, now backwards, now forwards, without taking the smallest interest in Dana's explanation, and occasionally putting his finger on some possibly conspicuous figure and saying 'What's that?'—rather as a child might exclaim 'Oh, look at that lovely big one there!' An earlier manager of his, Fitzroy Gardner, recorded that the expenses of running one show were considered uneconomical, something like £200 a performance, and Tree was begged to make retrenchments. He spent a day in going through the accounts, at last spotted a reasonable saving, and suggested that in future the theatre Green Room should be supplied with *The Daily Telegraph* instead of *The Times*, a saving of one shilling a week. Gardner once took him to task over his personal expenditure, saying that he ought not to lunch every day at the Carlton; whereupon Tree led Gardner across the road to a confectioner's shop, ordered him a bun and a glass of milk, and left him alone to practise what he preached; after which Gardner did not decline Tree's invitations to lunch at the Carlton. The combination of imaginative impulse and practical heedlessness in Tree's nature was demonstrated when he founded the Academy of Dramatic Art. He took two houses in Gower Street, furnished them, gave the institution his blessing, and left it to shift for itself.

Nothing but the huge success of many productions could have kept Tree out of the bankruptcy court; but with him Shakespeare was nearly always a box-office certainty. This was not solely due to his sumptuous presentations, but also to the excellent acting of his company and his wisdom in letting the other 'stars' shine. Sir Henry Irving, too, surrounded himself with good actors, but he used to cut their parts unmercifully to the grave detriment of the play, and people left his theatre thinking chiefly of his performance, and, because of her fascinating personality, Ellen Terry's. But Tree engaged the best possible actors and gave them every chance to make or increase their reputations. When he cast Lewis Waller for important parts at his new theatre, Shaw said that Waller was '*ten* times as good as the very best man' supporting Irving at the Lyceum. After Waller came Oscar Asche, then Lyn Harding, then Henry Ainley, then Matheson Lang, Robert Loraine, Owen Nares, and pretty well every first-class Shakespearean player of the age, whether for comedy (Lionel Brough) or for tragedy. The most versatile actor on the stage of my time was Lyn Harding, who during Tree's Festivals appeared in such widely diverse parts as Aguecheek in *Twelfth Night*, the Ghost in *Hamlet*, Cassius in *Julius Caesar*, Prospero in *The Tempest*, Ford in *The Merry Wives*, and Bolingbroke in *Richard II*, playing each in a masterly manner. Once he acted Tree and everyone else off the stage. He was Enobarbus in *Antony and Cleopatra*, and at the fiftieth performance the whole house cheered him. Tree continued to appear before the curtain taking all the calls meant for Harding, until at length the entire audience united in a single yell of 'HARDING', when the lights went up and the National Anthem was played. This cannot have been pleasant for Tree; but he maintained his policy of getting the best actors for the best parts and letting them speak as many of their lines as the spectacular mounting permitted. Sometimes he put on plays merely for the sake of exhibiting other artists to advantage, not appearing in them himself; for instance, *The Winter's Tale*, in which Ellen Terry gave an unforgettable performance as Hermione and Charles Warner made Leontes uncomfortably real. The cast of *The School for Scandal* at His Majesty's was a constellation of 'stars', but Tree's Sir Peter Teazle, though not one of his finest studies, was as good as any other performance in the play. When he revived *The Merry Wives* he took the risk of being obliterated in his own theatre by the charm of Ellen Terry as Mistress Page, the technique of Madge Kendal as Mistress Ford; and indeed Ellen Terry's performance would have made Shakespeare wonder whether he had unconsciously created a masterpiece, until he referred to the text and discovered that all the glory was in the personality of the actress.

Like many men of genius, from Shakespeare, who according to his friend Jonson 'flowed with that facility that sometime it was necessary he should be stopped', to Shaw, who could no more help clowning than preaching, Tree frequently released his abundant energy in outbursts of absurdity which disconcerted his solemn admirers. He was a born comedian, and enjoyed mystifying people, making them wonder whether he was serious or pulling their legs. The first time I met him personally, he suddenly asked me 'Have you ever been to Jerusalem?' I replied that I had not. 'How interesting!' he said. And a little later in the same evening he remarked 'Some day you must tell me why it was you didn't go to Jerusalem. It must have been a delightful experience—not to have gone there after all.' Humourless people were annoyed by this kind of thing, calling him a mere buffoon, but I quickly recognised it as the need of an actor to continue his performance off the stage, and my appreciation of it led to queer results; as when he insisted on my getting into a taxi with him one night and gave the following instructions to the driver: 'Drive us slowly round and round the West End until we tell you to stop. If you see a man in green trousers, a top hat and spotted waistcoat, blow your horn three times and increase your speed.' He then talked aimlessly about nothing in particular, saying amongst other things, though I had scarcely opened my mouth, that I must not interrupt him and that my tongue had been given me to hold it. Once an actor he knew well called to see him when he was made up for the part of Fagin. 'Who are you?' he demanded. The actor gave his name. 'Ah!' said Tree, 'forgive me. I didn't recognise you in my disguise.' Another actor applied to him for a part. Tree looked him carefully over, and then, instead of enquiring about his previous experience, asked 'How does your face freckle like that?'

I was the sole witness of a scene between him and an American press reporter. Tree was proposing to revisit the United States, and the reporter had called for an interview. We were in the dome of His Majesty's Theatre, where Tree had a banqueting-hall and a large sitting-room which he also used as a bedroom. Something the reporter said amused Tree, who instantly forgot business and made a burlesque speech about the United States. The moment the American perceived that a verbatim record of Tree's eloquent nonsense would get him the sack, he closed his notebook with a loud snap, reached for his hat, and got up. 'Thank you, Sir Tree, thank you very much', he said. 'You've got a fine place up here, but I hope you don't spend much time on the bal-cony outside. It's a long drop to the street, and they haven't got padded pavements—yet.' With which, and a curt 'good night', he left the room. 'How curious!' mused Tree, as the door closed with a bang. 'How curious! I never thought of that . . . Padded pavements! . . . The orange-peel would lose its terror.'

Nothing could stop him from playing the fool when in the mood. He was lunching one day with a friend at the Carlton Restaurant when he noticed someone alone at another table. Calling the waiter, he said 'My compliments to Mr Henry Arthur Jones—the gentleman lunching by himself over there—and will he very kindly come and speak to me for a minute?' I should add that he knew Henry Arthur Jones intimately, having produced several of his plays, though Jones, like Shaw, Brieux and other authors, had been driven in despair from the theatre by Tree's lack of method at rehearsals. The waiter returned to say that Tree was mistaken: the gentleman was not Mr Henry Arthur Jones. 'Yes, yes', said Tree, 'very funny, very funny indeed; he always did like his little joke. But this is important. Please tell Mr Jones that I should feel most grateful if he would behave seriously for once. I am very anxious to speak to him.' The waiter again addressed the solitary gentleman, who once more, with some severity, returned the statement that his name was not Jones. Whereupon Tree dismissed the waiter with a laugh which implied that Mr Jones was incorrigible. The lonely luncher finished his meal first, and on his way out stopped at Tree's table. 'I don't see why you should insist on knowing me', he said angrily. 'Surely it was enough to point out your mistake once.' 'Do you mean to tell me quite seriously that you are not my old friend Henry Arthur Jones?' queried Tree. 'I do, sir!' shouted the other. 'Then you were quite right to deny it', returned Tree mildly, and continued his lunch.

But he could be as witty as he enjoyed being silly, and some of his comments on people and things were unusually shrewd. A company of Sicilian actors, headed by Signor Grasso, were a nine-days wonder in London, and Tree went to see them in *Othello*. There was no restraint in Grasso's performance of the Moor, which was a sweeping, tornadic display of primitive and almost epileptic passion. In the great scenes of jealousy his eyes rolled in frenzy, he foamed at the mouth, and bellowed like a bull. 'Very fine, very remarkable', said Tree, 'but hardly Shakespeare's conception. You see, Grasso's Othello would never have wanted a pocket-handkerchief.' During the 1914–18 war the pantomimic comic opera *Chu-Chin-Chow* was produced by Oscar Asche at His Majesty's in Tree's absence. The dresses of the women in it were scanty and the atmosphere was voluptuous, providing the strongest possible contrast to the stern wartime conditions that prevailed outside the theatre. When Tree returned to town and saw the show, he dismissed it with the phrase 'More navel than millinery.'

Tree was the last of the great London actor-managers and a much richer character than any he assumed on the stage, except the Falstaff of *Henry IV*, which he could not act and therefore guyed. After his death the London theatres, with very few exceptions, were run by people who knew little about actors, less about acting, and nothing at all about the drama, and whose sole concern was to make as much money as possible in as short a time as they could. With all their faults the old actor-managers were the heirs of a noble tradition dating back to the time of Shakespeare. They respected their profession; they loved their work; their eyes were not always on the box-office; they kept alive the poetic drama; and the best Shakespearean actors were trained in their school.

Tree's annual Shakespeare Festivals would have been

impossible in a purely commercial theatre. He revived six or more of Shakespeare's plays within two or three weeks, each of them mounted superbly and acted magnificently by men and women who understood the art of speaking verse. He lost a lot of money on each Festival. In short he did the work of a National Subsidised Theatre; and with him a great epoch passed away.

Scene from *The School for Scandal*
eft to right)—Edward Terry as Crabtree ; Ellis Jeffreys as Lady Sneerwell ;
H. V. Esmond as Backbite ; Suzanne Sheldon as Mrs. Candour ;
Marie Löhr as Lady Teazle ; Tree as Sir Peter Teazle

Scene from Tree's production of Tolstoy's *Resurrection*
with Tree as Prince Dimitry ; Lily Brayton as Theodosia ;
Lena Ashwell as Katusha

Tree and Marie Löhr as
Sir Peter and Lady Teazle
in *The School for Scandal*

Tree as Wolsey and
Reginald Owen as Cromwell
in *Henry VIII*

Tree as
Colonel Newcome

Tree and Lily Hanbury in
1 *Bunch of Violets* by Sydney Grundy

Tree and Evelyn D'Alroy
in *The O'Flynn*

Tree as Nero in
Stephen Phillips's play

Tree as
Beethoven

Alexander as John Worthing
in a revival of *The Importance of Being Earnest* (1909)
by Oscar Wilde

SIR GEORGE ALEXANDER
(1858–1918)

THE most continuously successful actor-manager on the stage of my time was George Alexander, and throughout his tenancy of twenty-seven years the St James's Theatre was the most fashionable playhouse in London. The more expensive seats were occupied by Society with a capital 'S', the less expensive ones by those who longed to be in Society, the least expensive by those who wished to see what Society looked like. Under such circumstances it is not to be expected that the drama served up at the St James's Theatre was of the most exalted kind. Most of the plays dealt with life as lived by the upper classes, and peers of the realm were as common on the stage as they were in the stalls. Alexander catered for their dramatic taste much as the Savoy Hotel catered for their gastronomic taste; the dramas, like the dishes, were pleasant to the palate and left nothing disagreeable in the mind or the mouth. In a typical St James's play the humorous characters were delightfully playful, the serious characters charmingly sentimental, and the plot savoured of scandal without being objectionably truthful. Adultery was invariably touched on and inevitably touched up; theft was made thrilling, and murder romantic.

George Alexander himself was ideally suited to the parts he played and the dramas he produced: he was a polished but uninspired actor; he had a perfect sense of what his audiences wanted because it was exactly what *he* wanted; he was handsome in a rather expressionless way; his movements were as graceful as they were decorous; his voice was genteel and admirably modulated; and he was so well dressed that

23

men would often study his clothes before ordering their own. In private life, too, his appearance and behaviour were unexceptionable; his ordinary conversation among men could have been uttered with perfect propriety at any duchess's tea-party; he was calm, prudent, polite, and always pleasant. Until one got to know him intimately one would never suspect that he had any poetry, any deep feeling, in his nature. He was kind, not generous; likeable, not loveable; just, not indulgent; the last man to whom you would go for sympathy, the first man to whom you would go for advice. Yet that aloof manner and restrained behaviour concealed a very sensitive soul, which was revealed when he confessed to me that the older he grew the more nervous he felt at rehearsals.

As far as I know, only one person had the power to upset his almost invariable equanimity. This was Mrs Patrick Campbell, who made the hit of her career in the play which was perhaps the chief sensation of Alexander's management: *The Second Mrs Tanqueray* by Arthur Pinero, first seen in 1893. Mrs Campbell had the ability to make or mar a production. Rudolf Besier once told me that when, entirely due to the brilliance of her acting, his play *Lady Patricia* had been running to full houses for eight weeks, she suddenly took a dislike either to him or to her part—he was never quite sure which—and started fooling about on the stage, completely wrecking the show, which came off a few weeks later. She did not ruin *The Second Mrs Tanqueray*, partly because it was the talk of the town, partly because Alexander had a large personal following, and partly because she was at the commencement of her career and had to be cautious. But she ruined Alexander's good temper. He never forgot the experience, and except for a brief and very unpleasant association, which both of them did their best to forget, in *The Masqueraders*, a play by Henry Arthur Jones which followed *Tanqueray*, nearly eighteen years were to pass before she again appeared at the St James's, though in the interval he had half hoped, half feared that she would accept the part of Francesca in Stephen Phillips's poetic drama.

She was however the only actress on the stage who could play the lead in *Bella Donna*, a dramatic version by J. B. Fagan of a novel by Robert Hichens; Alexander engaged her for it in 1911; and, though it was an immense success, he assured me that he had never in his life felt so relieved as when the curtain finally descended on the last performance. Temperamental fits, violent scenes, infuriating incidents, were of common occurrence; and at last Alexander, unwilling to give her an opening for her wounding sarcasms, refused to speak to her, however intolerable such a state of things behind the curtain. Then, one evening, he was informed that she was letting down a scene with her stage-husband; so he decided to watch it from an unoccupied box. He could hardly believe his eyes. All through a very dramatic episode she was amusing herself by flicking chocolates against the backcloth, the tense conversation being punctuated by a series of 'plonks' as the chocolates hit what appeared to be a star-spangled sky and dropped with a dull thud into what was supposed to be the River Nile. Alexander was so furious that he forgot he was not on speaking terms with his leading lady, dashed back to the stage at the close of the scene, and rushed up to her. 'I see you are angry', she said. As he was clawing the air, gnashing his teeth, and almost inarticulate, this was a reasonable inference; and before he could utter a coherent phrase, she proceeded: 'Your wife would not like me to speak with you when you are angry. She says it upsets your digestion.' Marching past him, she went to her dressing-room, and locked the door. He wrote her a letter, which she returned unopened. In short, the long run of *Bella Donna* was a long agony for the manager, and I was not surprised to hear from Bernard Shaw that when he wrote *Pygmalion* for Alexander, with a wonderful part in it for Mrs Pat, the actor said to him: 'That play is a cert, a dead cert. Now listen to me. I will get you any actress you like to name for the flower girl. I will pay any salary she asks. You can settle your own terms. But go on for another play with Mrs Campbell I will *not*. I'd rather die.' Eventually the play was done by Beerbohm Tree, with Mrs Pat in the part of Eliza, and the rehearsals were so frightful that a set of photographs taken of Shaw immediately after were suppressed by him because he 'looked like an old dog who had been in a fight and got the worst of it'. Though Alexander would have been much better than Tree in the part of the professor, I have a feeling that he would have tried to make Shaw alter the phrase 'Not bloody likely!' to something less likely to fray the nerves of a fashionable St James's audience under his management.

A few years after the original production of *Bella Donna* I was with Alexander when he was thinking of reviving it, and he asked me to suggest someone for the leading part. I said that Mrs Pat was the only actress who could play it. 'Out of the question!' he exclaimed. 'She's quite impossible in the theatre, and makes my life a hell.' All the same he had to re-engage her, and when, during one of my wartime leaves, I saw the play, I went round for a chat with him during an interval. As I was saying 'good-bye' I remembered what he had told me and asked whether Mrs Pat was still impossible and whether his life was a hell. 'She is. It is', he replied with a gesture of despair. He engaged another actress for the film of *Tanqueray*, and so he was only compelled to rely on Mrs Campbell for two of the plays he revived.

Apart from those no theatre was ever run with such unruffled efficiency. Alexander was a model manager. He wasted neither time nor money. Rehearsals started on the minute at which they were called, and finished on the stroke

DRAWING-ROOM COMEDY

Alexander and Irene Vanbrugh
in *The Builder of Bridges* by Alfred Sutro

Alexander and Irene Vanbrugh
in *The Thief* by Henri Bernstein

Scene from Alexander's production of
Liberty Hall (1892) by R. C. Carton

Alexander (centre)
in *The Second Mrs. Tanqueray* (1893) by Arthur Pinero

Alexander as Bassanio
in Henry Irving's production
of *The Merchant of Venice*

Alexander as Prince Rudolf
in *The Prisoner of Zenda*
by Anthony Hope

Scene from Alexander's production
of *If I Were King* by Justin H. M'Carthy

Alexander and Irene Vanbrugh
in Pinero's *His House in Order*

Alexander in
D'Arcy of the Guards

Scene from Alexander's last production *The Aristocrat* (1917)
Alexander and Geneviève Ward both seated in centre

of the hour at which it was known they would be over. Actors were not kept hanging about while stage-managers argued with stage-carpenters and the producer discussed scenic effects with the painter. In the theatrical world of his time, whatever it may be now, his precision and punctuality were unique. There were no rushings and scurryings hither and thither because something had been forgotten or mislaid; there was no fuss, no bawling, no disputing, no heat, no hysteria. In my whole experience of him I never knew Alexander attempt to bully anyone; I never knew him to lose his temper or to be sarcastic at another's expense. He was always considerate, fair-minded, tactful and helpful. Anyone who thinks such virtues commonplace has no conception of life behind the scenes of a theatre during rehearsals, which frequently resembles that of a zoo with most of the wild animals at large.

George Alexander Gibb Samson, to give his full name before he dispensed with the less imposing half of it, started to earn a living at fifteen as a clerk in a draper's warehouse. While engaged there he became a keen amateur actor and went on the stage at the age of twenty-one, much to the annoyance of his father, who was in the dry-goods trade and thought the lad was descending in the social scale. Almost at once he was cast for leading juvenile parts, and within two years had secured an engagement with Henry Irving. In 1885 Irving produced *Faust* at the Lyceum, casting Alexander for the part of Valentine. But H. B. Conway, who played Faust, left the company after four performances, and Alexander made his name by playing the part for the rest of the run. In 1890 he went into management at the Avenue Theatre (where the Playhouse now is), moving on to the St James's a year later, and obtaining a permanent position in the West End in 1892 with the production of *Lady Windermere's Fan* by Oscar Wilde. He experienced great difficulty in persuading Wilde to write his first comedy. First of all he bribed him with an advance on royalties; then he badgered him with letters; but whenever they met Wilde said 'I am in what I call the invention period', and would not make any promises. At last it was written and Wilde read it to Alexander, who said he would produce it at once. 'What about terms?' asked the author: 'I'm always in want of money, you know.' Alexander promptly offered to buy the play outright for £1000. 'That is a very very large amount', said Wilde. 'A thousand pounds. It seems almost too good to believe.' He paused for reflection, and then displayed his shrewdness: 'I have so much confidence in your excellent judgment, my dear Alec, that I cannot but refuse your generous offer.' The original run brought him £7000.

Three years later Alexander did Wilde's last comedy, *The Importance of Being Earnest*, out of which, by regular revivals, he made more money than from anything he produced except *His House in Order* and *Bella Donna*, both of which however had the advantage of long runs on their first appearance. But the trial of Wilde cut short the original run of *Earnest*, and, barring a brief revival in 1902, fifteen years elapsed before it was put on as a stop-gap, took the town by storm, and lasted nearly a year. It was written in two or three weeks and apparently with the ease of complete spontaneity, because Alexander told me that when he asked Wilde to omit a scene the author protested in these terms: 'This scene which you feel is superfluous cost me terrible exhausting labour and heart-rending nerve-racking strain. You may not believe me, but I assure you on my honour that it must have taken fully five minutes to write.'

Wilde once complained that George Alexander did not act on the stage: he behaved. If so, he behaved extraordinarily well as John Worthing in *The Importance of Being Earnest*, for no other actor has come within measurable distance of him in that part. As a matter of fact he was full of histrionic intelligence and never made a mistake in casting. What he lacked was the sort of intelligence that could perceive a good play outside the dramatic convention of the time. But in that respect he was just the same as the other managers, none of whom recognised Shaw as a money-making playwright. When Alexander read *Candida* he confessed to the author that he would like to play Marchbanks if only the poet were made blind to gain the sympathy of the audience; and after reading *You Never Can Tell* he wrote: 'When I got to the end, I had no more idea what you meant by it than a tom cat.' Twelve years later he and his fellow-managers changed their tune, but that was simply because an uncommercial management, Granville-Barker's, had shown that Shaw's plays were a sound commercial proposition.

One of Alexander's biggest successes in the nineties was *The Prisoner of Zenda*, and in those days he was the leading matinée idol (as it was called) of the metropolis, a position he held unchallengeably until Lewis Waller produced *Monsieur Beaucaire* early in the present century. I happened to be with Alexander about three years before his death, and remarked favourably one day on the length of the pit queue. 'Ah!' he sighed, 'you would not say that if you had been with me in *The Prisoner of Zenda*. Then the queues stretched into St James's Street.' He also did the sequel to *Zenda*, called *Rupert of Hentzau*, which failed because the hero is killed and the play ends with his body lying in state. 'I should have known', said Alexander to me, 'that audiences don't mind seeing the hero die, but dislike seeing him dead.' 'Why didn't you bring him back to life?' I asked. 'Anything can happen in a melodrama.' 'Not at the St James's', he gravely replied.

Though he had to abdicate his position as London's most popular *jeune premier*, his management remained almost uniformly successful; and when I first saw him in 1906 he was setting the fashion for soft collars with lounge suits in Pinero's play *His House in Order*, the original production of which ran longer than any of his previous pieces. Alexander had a profound respect for Pinero, who produced his own plays and whose prestige was so vast that for many years he was a sort of stage-dictator. If he sent a play to a manager, it just had to be produced: no one had the courage to reject it: and even though a failure it had to be kept running for a certain number of weeks. Gerald Du Maurier once said that his early years as a manager were clouded by the fact that every morning when he went to the theatre he was in fear and trembling lest a new play had arrived from Sir Arthur Pinero. Alexander must have suffered considerable discomfort when he received *The Thunderbolt* and *Mid-Channel* from Pinero. Though he admired them, he guessed they would fail, as indeed they did, but the possibility of being struck by the first and sunk in the second was less terrifying than the certainty of their author's wrath had they been rejected.

At rehearsals Alexander was like a child in the hands of Pinero, whose commands were received as if delivered from Mount Sinai. He was mad on details, telling actors exactly how to move, what gestures to make, precisely where and when to stand or sit, how to stress words; and as he knew his plays by heart, there was trouble if an actor changed a word or slurred over a syllable or ignored the punctuation of the text by making too long or too short a pause. I believe that Alexander stood in awe of Pinero, because I heard him say that he dared not suggest an alteration which he knew would improve one of the dictator's plays. Incidentally Pinero, who had been one himself, hated actors. His career is the best instance on record of how far talent and industry will take a man without a suspicion of genius. While Oscar Wilde would toss off a comedy in a month, and Bernard Shaw would finish one in six weeks, Pinero would work like a beaver for a year at one of his carefully constructed pieces, which, when finished, might have been written by any of his talented and industrious contemporaries; and he became the leading dramatist of an age that dismissed Wilde as a charlatan and Shaw as a clown.

Very rarely did Alexander depart from his cautious policy of doing conventional modern work of the Pineronic pattern at the St James's Theatre; but in the nineties he revived two of Shakespeare's most respectable comedies, *As You Like It* and *Much Ado About Nothing*; and in 1902 he produced *Paolo and Francesca* by Stephen Phillips, the only English poet since Shakespeare who has written highly successful and dramatically effective blank verse plays.

But Alexander's uniqueness was not manifested in his own acting nor in the plays he produced. He really excelled as a man of affairs, perhaps the only man in history who ever ran a theatre without a hitch and under whom actors could feel secure from botheration. This extraordinary gift also found expression when he represented South St Pancras on the London County Council from 1907 till 1913, and would have been invaluable in the House of Commons if parliamentary procedure had enabled him to use it. I served under him on several committees, and therefore speak from experience when I say that he made a flawless chairman. Most theatrical committees, as I knew them, were self-admiration associations, the chief thing about them being the unlimited love each member had for himself and his own obsolete or obstructive ideas. In fairness I am bound to add that, without Alexander, their sessions, though lengthy, were extremely entertaining; but that, with him, they were brief, businesslike, and quite uninteresting. He introduced method and application into a world of glorified footledom. His idea when attending a committee meeting was that something had to be done, and he did it. Other people felt that something ought to be talked about, and they chattered—mostly about themselves.

It so happened that I worked with him on what he described as the stiffest job of that sort he had ever tackled: the organising committee for the Shakespeare Tercentenary Performance at Drury Lane Theatre in 1916, of which he was chairman and I was secretary. Every leading actor of the day was on that committee, though Tree, the President, being in America, could not attend the meetings; and as nearly every leading actor wanted to play nearly every leading part, Alexander had to use considerable tact, patience and skill to prevent explosions. While suffering from the disease which killed him two years later, he worked unceasingly and never once displayed irritation. His habitual courtesy and suavity did not desert him for a moment; though he had to deal with actors who felt they were being slighted by the offer of parts beneath their dignity, musicians who considered their compositions more worthy of the occasion than those of their fellow-artists, authors who believed their reputations demanded better seats in the theatre than those provided for them, painters who had notions of design and decoration that were infinitely superior to anything of the sort ever seen on the stage, peers who insisted on their rights, and programme-sellers who harped on their wrongs.

Alexander's social imperturbability was matched by his business acumen and unfailing common sense. I never knew him give an opinion that did not make the opinions of others seem silly; and, to do them justice, they usually followed his advice after giving vent to a certain amount of froth and nonsense. He was a born statesman and diplomat, and could have run a country as easily as a company. But the unreality of politics would have jarred on a man who took the art of acting seriously.

SIR FRANK BENSON
(1858–1939)

UNLIKE the other famous actor-managers of his time, Frank Benson was practically untrained when he began to play leading parts. His career opened too auspiciously. While at New College, Oxford, he produced the *Agamemnon* of Aeschylus in the original Greek, and was complimented upon it by prominent people in all walks of life, Gladstone, Tennyson, Browning, Henry Irving and Ellen Terry prophesying future renown for the daring undergraduate. And as, that same year, he won the three-mile race in the inter-University Sports in record time, he made a reputation in the athletic and aesthetic worlds which was to have considerable influence on his work.

His next public act was to produce *Romeo and Juliet* in London with a company of amateurs; after which Henry Irving engaged him for the part of Paris in the Lyceum production of that play (1882). Advised to get some experience in the provinces, he joined a Shakespearean touring company, which was soon left stranded because the manager and chief actor, unwilling to meet his creditors, suddenly decamped. Fortunately Benson's father was well-off, and sent young Frank enough money to buy the wardrobe and scenery and to start on tour as the F. R. Benson Company in 1883. The rest of his life was spent in adding to his Shakespearean repertory and taking the plays all over the United Kingdom. He became an institution in the land, generation after generation of British schoolboys grounding their knowledge of Shakespeare as a dramatist on his performances. I was one of them, and I remain grateful to him for making Shakespeare, whom

3

I found intolerably tedious at school, appear wonderful and mysterious on the stage. Especially mysterious, I am bound to add, because his acting of the great tragic rôles made them largely incomprehensible. He mouthed the lines until they were meaningless, sang them until they were indistinguishable and bawled them until they were deafening. But it all sounded magnificent when one was fourteen years of age, and it was a delightful change from the prosaic business of recitation in the class-room. He had nearly every fault of which an actor can be guilty: when he spoke verse he ranted, and when he spoke prose he rattled; but these mannerisms must have increased with the years, because, being his own manager and producer, there was no one to check them. Nevertheless his performances were thoroughly enjoyable. They were bustling affairs, full of energy and excitement; his companies were first-rate; and the stage-fights were thrillingly realistic.

He was greatly helped at the outset of his career by a general belief that he was closely related to the then Archbishop of Canterbury, and it cannot have pleased his business-manager when an irreverent critic known as Corno di Bassetto went to see his production of *A Midsummer Night's Dream* early in 1890, learnt from someone who knew Benson well that the archiepiscopal relationship was a pure invention of the press, and informed his readers that 'My first impulse on hearing this was, I own, to demand my money back.' It did not help matters when a couple of stalls were sent by the management to Bassetto with the statement that 'evening dress was indispensable', because that irrepressible critic, who later became known as 'G.B.S.', promptly stated in an article that he refused to don what he called a 'class uniform' and the attempt to compel him to do so made him half suspect that Benson was a relative of the Archbishop after all.

But what helped Benson more than his connection with the

whole hierarchy would have done was his all-round sportsmanship. Everyone felt that Shakespeare was safe in the hands of one who could play cricket, tennis, football and hockey so well, who went in for rowing and running and water-polo, and who would break the ice and enjoy a swim between a matinée of *Hamlet* and an evening performance of *Richard III*. His company backed these deeds of hardihood, and it was rumoured that a sound bowler or a dependable half-back had a better chance of becoming a Bensonian than a good actor. In such an atmosphere of athletics it was only to be expected that wherever possible the muscles of the company would be exercised on the stage, and the most memorable moments in a Benson production were the skirmishes. Though the dialogue makes it clear that the doctor and parson in *The Merry Wives of Windsor* do not come to blows, Benson had a terrific all-in combat which brightened up the play considerably; and when Shakespeare was considerate enough to allow him a duel, as with Richmond at the end of *Richard III*, it lasted some minutes, battle-axes giving way to swords, swords to daggers, sparks flying, shields crashing, breasts heaving, eyes flashing, and a growing conviction in the audience that the houses of York and Lancaster were done for and the throne of England would shortly be vacant.

Apart from such exhibitions, Benson indulged in many acrobatic feats on the stage. His Petruchio jumped tables, bounded through windows, and flung his future wife over his shoulders as the ordinary man would fling a cloak. As Caliban he entered with a real fish in his mouth, carried weights that would have broken most people's backs, swarmed up a tree, hung suspended from its branches by his toes, and made headlong descents down a rope from the flies. Ill-health did not deter him from such exploits, and he once played Richard III with a temperature of 104. He was aware that gymnastics were a too prominent feature of his performances, and even admitted that he was inclined 'to make muscular activity do duty for mental perception'.

It cannot truthfully be said that he gave a really good performance of any big Shakespearean part, but he was extremely funny as Dr Caius in *The Merry Wives*, and very entertaining as Young Marlow in Goldsmith's *She Stoops to Conquer*; which suggests that if he had been properly trained he might have made an excellent comedian. On the other hand his Macbeth was so appallingly bad that no training on earth could have made it passably good. I had seen him in nearly all his leading rôles when I came across a criticism which implied that the high spot of his career was Richard II. Not having seen him in that part, I wrote asking him to play it on his next visit to Bedford. He replied that he would, and I went down to see it. Alas! it was deplorable, and I had not the heart to go round to his dressing-room afterwards and thank him for all the trouble he had taken.

But this episode gives the key-note of his character. He was a very kind-hearted and sweet-natured man, who would do anything he could to oblige people or to help them. The members of his company adored him and more than once volunteered to play for half their salaries in order to help him through difficult times. I doubt if any manager has been so popular with his fellow-artists. The charm of his personality was such that no one could do too much for him. He was often financially embarrassed, but the people who advanced money to tide him over found it impossible to remind him of what he owed them. Harold V. Neilson, who was once an actor in his company and eventually became his manager, said that 'When Benson dies he will be followed to the grave by five thousand creditors, all of whom will shed a tear because they cannot lend him a bit more.' His money-troubles were not due to personal extravagance or luxurious living. His habits were spartan. When *The Merry Wives* drew a record house in Manchester, Neilson suggested a celebration at the Midland Hotel. 'Certainly', said Benson: 'I'll have spinach and rice pudding.' His notion of enjoying himself when not acting or playing a game was to spend half an hour at an open window swinging dumb-bells or Indian-clubs. Though well above the active-service age, he served in a French ambulance unit during the 1914–18 war, and won the Croix de Guerre. The last time I saw him, when he was seventy-seven years of age, he was running up Regent Street against the road traffic.

His frequent need of money was due to his idealism. He wished to inoculate the country with Shakespeare, and for this purpose he was not content to exploit the success of this or that production. Twice in London he wrecked his chances of establishing himself as a West End manager by taking off a play that was making money and substituting his repertory. He never considered the box-office when it interfered with his desire to do more and yet more Shakespeare. At one time he had three companies on the road, and he was the only actor-manager in theatrical history to produce as many as thirty-five of Shakespeare's plays (the exceptions being *Titus Andronicus* and *Troilus and Cressida*), and the first actor to perform the complete text of *Hamlet*. For some thirty years, from 1891 to 1919 continuously, he was responsible for the Annual Festivals at Stratford-on-Avon; and as they had developed, under his direction, from a small local affair into an international celebration, he should have been allowed to continue there until his voluntary retirement; but he became the casualty of a committee, the victim of others' vanity. True, he received the freedom of the borough of Stratford-on-Avon in 1910, an honour which had only been bestowed on one other actor, David Garrick, in 1769; but as he had spent the whole of his personal fortune in staging the works of the man by whose name Stratford has thriven, the ratepayers ought to have maintained him in comfort for life instead of leaving him to die on a civil list pension of £100 a year.

His love of Shakespeare made him enthusiastic about everything he associated with the rollicking days of Queen Elizabeth; pageantry, heraldry, Morris dancing, street processions, banner-waving, folk-songs, etc.; and he tried to bring all this on to the stage. In fact his dreams and pre-occupations as a producer were on such a scale that he never found time to study his parts carefully, and used to misquote and transpose lines with a freedom that would have made Shakespeare peevish. The train of thought in his public speeches suffered from a similar absence of mind. I once heard him give an address in Southwark Cathedral, quite clearly and eloquently, but at the conclusion of his discourse, which lasted an hour, I had not the faintest idea of what he had said, and I am quite certain that he was equally in the dark. At a Stratford dinner in his honour, he began his reply to the toast 'I don't know what all this is about—it's all very flattering and wonderful— but I don't know what it's about . . .' and then spoke for half an hour, leaving his distinguished audience also to wonder what it was about.

Benson was a terrific worker, and frequently rehearsed his company for six or seven hours at a stretch until they were exhausted, following which he played a leading part as freshly as if he had been asleep all day. He seemed tireless, and would add to his labours many feats of organisation which other men would have considered full-time jobs. He did more than anyone else to establish the Actors Association, which guarded the interests of the profession, and even persuaded Sir Henry Irving, who began by opposing the movement,

Benson as Richard III

Benson as Richard II

F. R. and Mrs. Benson as Macbeth and Lady Macbeth

Benson as Antony in *Antony and Cleopatra* (1894)

Scene from Benson's production of *Richard III*

Scene from Benson's production of *The Taming of the Shrew*

to become its first President. When the Actors Association became too much like a trade union, Benson was equally energetic in helping to found the Stage Guild to take its place; and in connection with this I experienced the exceptional politeness and tact which were part of his charm. Godfrey Tearle wanted me to become the secretary of the Guild, and some time in 1924 I went along to interview the committee of managers. But I quickly became embroiled in an angry argument with one of them, Percy Hutchison, and was on the point of cursing the whole set-up and walking out when Benson intervened in such a soothing and conciliatory manner that I forced back the words which were about to flow from me and the interview proceeded and terminated harmoniously, though my insistence on my own freedom prevented me from getting the job.

Because of his alluring social qualities, no less than his infectious enthusiasm, Benson was eminently qualified to represent his profession. And, moreover, his company was the best school of acting in his time. He could boast in the year 1920 that about seventy Old Bensonians were playing prominent parts in the London theatres. Nearly all the first-class Shakespearean actors in the country between 1890 and 1930 learnt their business under him; for instance, Oscar Asche, Matheson Lang, Henry Ainley, Baliol Holloway; and others who were famous before his time were proud to act with him, such as George Weir, a great Shakespearean clown, and Geneviève Ward, whose Volumnia in *Coriolanus* and Queen Margaret in *Richard III* were masterpieces in the grand tragic style associated with Sarah Siddons.

As he had spent so much of his life in the provinces, Benson was unknown in the circles where people have to move if they covet distinctions; and George Alexander told me that when he put forward Benson's name for a knighthood he was asked to give an account of his work and explain why he should be honoured, since the people in the Lord Chamberlain's office seemed to know nothing about him. Yet no one in the history of the stage had deserved public recognition of his services so richly as Benson; and when he was knighted by George V at Drury Lane Theatre, immediately after his appearance as Julius Caesar in the Shakespeare Tercentenary Performance of 1916, not a member of his profession felt envious.

Benson as Charles Surface
in *The School for Scandal*

Benson starts touring
(1883)

Benson as Caliban
in *The Tempest*

Benson as Petruchio
in *The Taming of the Shrew*

Waller and
Evelyn Millard
in Conan Doyle's
Brigadier Gerard

Waller and
C. W. Somerset
as Captain and
Sir Anthony Absolute
in *The Rivals*

LEWIS WALLER
(1860–1915)

THE two best male voices I have heard on the stage were those of Forbes-Robertson and Lewis Waller, but they were quite different from one another. Robertson's was musical, melodious, melancholy, beautiful, likened by Shaw to the chalumeau register of a clarionet. Waller's rang through the theatre like a bell and stirred like a trumpet. With Robertson, as with Ellen Terry, one felt that their native language was the same as Shakespeare's. With Waller, as with Geneviève Ward, one felt that Shakespeare's verse was a tremendous instrument and that they knew how to wield it. Vocally speaking, there can never have been a finer Henry V, a more striking Hotspur, than Waller's. He was the ideal actor of heroic parts, and throughout the first decade of this century he was the most popular figure on the English stage. It may be doubted whether any player in history has had such a large and fanatical female following. This was due not only to his good looks but to his virile acting and his vibrant voice.

The scenes at his first and last nights had to be seen and heard to be believed. The pit and gallery, mostly filled with women, went completely mad. These ladies banded themselves into a club or society vulgarly known as the K.O.W. (Keen on Waller) Brigade, and they packed the pit at almost every performance. Waller's first appearance in a play was received with such a storm of shouts and yells and hand-clapping and foot-stamping that the action was often held up for several minutes. I remember being present at the last performance of his Othello, when for over half an hour the curtain went up and down to the accompaniment of hysterical howls for a speech and other noises that would not have been out of place in a menagerie. Most of the plays he produced were exactly suited to this class of demonstration. I saw him in a melodrama called *The Duke's Motto* fighting his way single-handed up a narrow stairway against apparently insuperable odds and leaving a trail of expiring swordsmen in his wake. It was good tough stuff, and everyone but the highly sophisticated enjoyed it; but the puerile nature of the plays he usually put on, and the adolescent behaviour of his female admirers, prevented many people from appreciating his superb gift as a declaimer of Shakespeare's rhetoric, and frequently exposed him to ridicule. He was aware of this, and made the best of it. He once told me that he loved Shakespeare and never wanted to act in the plays of anyone else.

'Then why not go on producing Shakespeare?' I said.

'I would if I could but I can't', he replied. 'If only I could pay my way, without a cent of profit, I'd stick to Shakespeare. But it's no good. The public want *Robin Hood* and *Monsieur Beaucaire*; and after all I must live.'

'But what about your crowd of female worshippers? Surely they come regularly to whatever you put on? Their taste in plays is catholic. So long as you are in them, they'll be content with anything, from *Hamlet* to *Charley's Aunt*.'

Waller smiled while I was speaking. Then he became grave, and answered my questions with two more: 'Will no one rid me of these turbulent priestesses? . . . Besides, what shall it profit a manager if he fill the whole pit and has to paper his stalls?'

Like so many actors, Waller did not care for the parts in which he was chiefly admired. He told me that, except for Shakespeare, he would rather play in the class of light comedy then associated with Sir Charles Wyndham. It may have been

Waller in *A White Man*

Scene from Waller's production of Conan Doyle's *The Fires of Fate*
(Waller on right)

Waller in *The Duke's Motto*

Waller and Evelyn Millard in *Monsieur Beaucaire*

Scene from Waller's production of *The Three Musketeers*
(Waller, as D'Artagnan, second **from left**)

Waller and Madge Titheradge
in *Bardelys the Magnificent*

Waller and Grace Lane
in *Miss Elizabeth's Prisoner*

Waller and Evelyn Millard
in *The Harlequin King*

Waller and Evelyn Millard as
Brutus and Portia in Tree's production
of *Julius Caesar* (1898)

Waller and Evelyn Millard
as Othello and Desdemona

Waller as
Henry V

Waller and Evelyn Millard as Romeo and Juliet

because he fancied himself in the wrong sort of part that he was never given a good part of any kind during his period as an amateur actor. For some five years he was foreign correspondence clerk in the city firm of his uncle; after which he changed his name from Waller Lewis to Lewis Waller and became a professional actor at the age of twenty-three. Following a succession of juvenile parts, he went into management and toured the provinces with *A Woman of No Importance*, Oscar Wilde's second comedy, which Tree had successfully done at the Haymarket Theatre. Wilde attended one of the rehearsals and Waller wanted to know whether Tree's part suited him. 'You make it suit you', said Wilde, not wishing to upset him. But Waller knew that a cynical roué was hardly in his style, felt that Wilde was merely being kind, and pressed for an honest opinion. 'I think you are so good', said Wilde, 'that no one except myself will know that the part was not written for you. But between ourselves, my dear fellow, I long to see you as Milton's Samson Agonistes. . . . Now come and have supper with me. I long for that too.' Waller also produced *An Ideal Husband* at the Haymarket Theatre in 1895 and played the leading character, Sir Robert Chiltern. He did better with this, but I heard that Wilde's sole comment on his performance was: 'He would make an admirable D'Artagnan.' A sound prophecy, for about five years later Waller played that part in *The Three Musketeers* and made one of the hits of his life.

When Tree opened Her Majesty's Theatre in 1897 a leading member of his company was Waller, who, although he had scored several successes as a romantic lover before then, first became the adored of all adorers as Brutus in *Julius Caesar* (1898). Bernard Shaw did not think much of him in the part, but everyone else thought a lot; and when he played the Bastard in Tree's production of *King John* the following year, the yells for 'Waller' made Tree realise that they had better separate. Waller realised it too, and in 1900 he rented the Lyceum Theatre, where he produced *The Three Musketeers* and made a sensational hit with *Henry V*. He was forty years old, and so complete was his success that it looked as if he, rather than Tree, would carry on the work of Irving and give the best Shakespearean revivals of his time. But Waller was fond of a quiet life in comfortable surroundings. Unlike the majority of 'star' actors, then and now, he never turned up at big social functions, never associated himself with charities or movements of any sort, and preferred a game of golf to Green Room gossip. I once saw him at a committee meeting, but I am quite sure his presence was due to a mistake, for he was dressed in tweeds with a pink tie, sat still without opening his mouth for ten minutes, and then slipped noise-lessly away, with the look of a man who is determined to reduce his handicap.

William Mollison told me that as a small boy he was in his father's dressing-room one night during the original run of Waller's *Henry V*. It was the night when Queen Victoria's death was announced, and Waller entered Mollison's dressing-room with a face of grief, suddenly bursting into tears and crying 'She's dead, Bill, she's dead!' Mollison tried to comfort him and begged him not to take it too much to heart. But Waller was inconsolable. 'It's the receipts, Bill', he sobbed: 'the receipts are bound to drop.' They did.

The production of *Henry V*, though enormously successful for Shakespeare, was not successful enough for Waller, who wanted a 'winner' that would always win; and at length he got it with *Monsieur Beaucaire*, which was produced at the Comedy Theatre in October 1902 and enjoyed a run of 430 performances. Nearly all the actor-managers of those days had one or two plays which they could rely upon for a revival when other plays failed them. Charles Wyndham had *David Garrick*, John Hare *A Pair of Spectacles*, Tree had *Trilby*, Alexander *The Importance of Being Earnest*, Martin-Harvey *The Only Way*, Forbes-Robertson *Hamlet*, Fred Terry *The Scarlet Pimpernel*, Oscar Asche *The Taming of the Shrew*, and Lewis Waller had *Monsieur Beaucaire*, in which the French hero scores off his English rivals in that wittily gallant fashion so dear to romantic Englishwomen. 'Pitiful stroller! born in a stable', cries one of these British cads. 'Is it not an honour to have been born where monsieur so evidently was bred?' returns Beaucaire with a low bow, and the ladies in the audience squeal with delight. 'Thank heaven I wasn't born a Frenchman!' exclaims another bestial islander. 'Monsieur', comes the suave response, 'permit me to send my thanks to heaven with yours', and his feminine admirers can scarcely contain themselves. In brief, the play was a perfect vehicle for Waller's more commonplace gifts, and for the rest of his life he merely had to revive it in order to repay him for his failures.

Its success enabled him to take the Imperial Theatre in Westminster, where among other things he produced *Romeo and Juliet*, in which the death of the hero was more than his adorers could stand, and they refused to witness such an impious proceeding. *Brigadier Gerard* was more to their taste; but it did not repeat the success of *Beaucaire* because the chief character was more of a boy's hero than a lady's man. His three years at the Imperial were followed by four years at the Lyric Theatre, where he revived *Henry V*, acted Hotspur in *Henry IV*, Part I, for a few matinées, appeared as Captain Absolute in *The Rivals*, and, with H. B. Irving as Iago, Evelyn Millard as Desdemona, Henry Ainley as Cassio, and himself as the Moor, gave the best all-round representation of *Othello* within my memory.

45

During a stage career of thirty-two years he played about two hundred parts without missing a single performance, which must have been a record; and he was commanded five times to appear before King Edward VII at Windsor and Sandringham, which must have been another record. But his most significant record was not of his own making: the creation of a cult, which I am told has been repeated and extended since then among filmgoers, but the like of which had not been known before his time in the world of entertainment. There had of course been matinée idols like George Alexander, Johnston Forbes-Robertson and William Terriss; but Waller was more like a god than an idol, and Waller-worship was akin to divine service: it was blasphemy to suggest that he was not perfect, profanation to imply that there were other gods than he. To illustrate this aspect of female infatuation, Lady Benson used to tell a story. After she had been playing Princess Katharine to Lewis Waller's Henry V, a female member of the Benson company came to her dressing-room and asked 'May I kiss you?' Assuming it to be a tribute to her performance of the French Princess, she consented, received a warm kiss on the lips, and a few words of explanation: 'Thank you so much. I shall never be kissed by Lewis Waller, but he has just kissed you as "Katharine", and that's as near to the real thing as I shall ever get.'

The effect of this absurd adulation on a simple, agreeable, jolly, and wholly unaffected fellow like Waller was that he felt amused, irritated, pleased and ashamed in about equal proportions. 'How sweet of you!' he said one evening to a girl who brought him a thank-offering. 'Silly little fool!' he remarked to a friend as she left the room. Certainly he did not deserve such worshippers, for he was a splendid actor.

SIR JOHN MARTIN-HARVEY
(1863–1944)

IF one man more than another stood out in those days as a typical actor of the old school, the last eminent specimen of a rapidly disappearing class, he was John Martin-Harvey, the only manager whom no one could possibly have mistaken for anything but an actor, whether in the ball-room, on the tennis courts, at a morning reception, or in the street. He always seemed to be playing a part, and when he came into a room he 'made an entrance'. This was in some degree due to his lifelong reverence for Sir Henry Irving, who, whatever he may have been as an actor, was an outstanding personality whose mere presence could be felt in a crowd of notabilities. Harvey liked to think that the mantle of Elijah-Irving had fallen on the shoulders of Elisha-Harvey, and this gave him a continuous consciousness of his own deportment. I have seen him at committee meetings, silent, gloomy, cogitative, self-absorbed; and when called upon for his opinion, he gave it in a few solemn words accompanied by an ample impressive wave of the hand. I am not saying that he could not throw off this stagey manner among intimate friends and in the bosom of his family, but I never saw him in a perfectly natural and genial mood, and I am describing him as he appeared in public and among his managerial contemporaries. One remark he made to Lewis Waller has remained in my memory for nearly forty years. Waller was talking about the necessity of playing down to the public taste if a manager wished to keep a balance in the bank. Harvey, with a regal gesture, spoke grandiloquently into the air: 'I always give the public of my best: it is their due, and my prerogative.' He really meant this, because even the second-rate melodramas which he sometimes produced were, in his opinion, worthy instruments of the actor's art.

As a youngster Martin-Harvey entered his family's firm as a shipwright, but he was bored with the work and wanted to be a painter. Suddenly he became keen on the stage; his father paid for him to have lessons in elocution; and an introduction to Henry Irving got him a job at the Lyceum Theatre when he was nineteen years of age. It happened that he joined the company for the production of *Romeo and Juliet* in which F. R. Benson was engaged for the part of Paris; but Harvey was a mere 'walker-on' and had to content himself with walking on and off the stage for many seasons without opening his mouth except to make noises with the rest of the crowd. He was an ambitious youth, and this kind of silent acting made him discontented; so with a few other fellows in the same quandary he formed a company and started a series of summer tours when the Lyceum was closed. Thus he gained experience as an actor in all sorts of characters. Even so, as time went on and he got no further with Irving than playing parts of a few lines, he began to feel that he was a failure and again turned his attention to painting, which he studied at Heatherley's School of Art. Perhaps if he had not married at an early age he might have left the Lyceum, but the salary was regular, the vacation tours were helpful, and his admiration for his master, Irving, increased instead of diminishing as he became more disheartened over his prospects.

After some fourteen years of thwarted endeavour at the Lyceum, he left, and very soon made an impression as Pelléas to the Mélisande of Mrs Patrick Campbell in Maeterlinck's play (1898). Then came *The Only Way*, a dramatic version of Dickens's novel *A Tale of Two Cities*, in which he made the

Martin-Harvey
as Richard III

Martin-Harvey as Sir Dagonet
in Henry Irving's production
of *King Arthur* (1895)

Martin-Harvey and N. de Silva
as Hamlet and Ophelia

Scene from Reinhardt's production at Covent Gar

Edipus Rex, with Martin-Harvey in the name-part

Martin-Harvey and N. de Silva
in *The Breed of the Treshams*

Martin-Harvey as Sydney Carton
in *The Only Way*

Scene from Martin-Harvey's production of *The Breed of the Treshams*

hit of his career as Sydney Carton. His success both as actor and manager was founded on this play, which was written at the suggestion of his wife. They were touring America in Irving's company early in 1895, and while at Saint Louis they went for a trip into the country. Returning in an open tramcar, they were wondering how to start a company of their own. 'We must have a play which will appeal to all humanity', said Harvey. 'Then you must do *A Tale of Two Cities* and play Sydney Carton', said his wife. 'There have been several plays on that subject and they have not succeeded', said he. 'Because they were not good plays: we must make a better one', said she. They got off the tramcar, bought a copy of Dickens's novel, and started to make notes for the drama in Chicago a week later. In the following years they gave every minute of their spare time to its construction, and then, having worked out the plot in detail, they asked a clergyman, who had done this sort of thing before, to write the dialogue. The clergyman's early efforts were not successful, but soon a better hand appeared in the writing, and eventually the Harveys learnt that the first clergyman had obtained the assistance of another clergyman.

After many vicissitudes, and with the financial backing of a well-known Shakespearean reader named J. H. Leigh, *The Only Way* was produced at the Lyceum during Irving's temporary absence in 1899, and was soon the most discussed play of the season. But it lost money; and even during a tour of the provinces it created enthusiasm but failed to cover expenses. When, a little later, Harvey produced *A Cigarette Maker's Romance* in London, the same thing happened. There was, he said, 'much enthusiasm, every appearance of prosperity, meagre returns, a wide belief that we were becoming the richest people in the profession, and a dread of the butcher's bill'. After that they were on the rocks, and he had to pawn his watch just before, as a last hope, he tried a second tour of *The Only Way*. This was enormously successful, and thenceforward they were on velvet, the play becoming the most prosperous stage adaptation of a literary masterpiece on record. Another big provincial draw was *The Breed of the Treshams*, which was sent him during his first American tour as a 'star', and which he liked so much that he wanted to meet the author 'John Rutherford', whom he pictured, from the stirring dialogue, to be a pretty tough fellow. Two handsome ladies walked into his hotel at Ottawa and announced that they were 'John Rutherford'; so his chief money-makers were written, the first by two clergymen, the second by two women.

But Martin-Harvey was not content to live in comfort on his box-office successes, and gradually added to his repertory four of Shakespeare's plays—*Hamlet, Richard III, The Taming of the Shrew* and *Henry V*—two of Maeterlinck's—*Pelléas and Mélisande* and *The Burgomaster of Stilemonde*—and *Oedipus Rex* by Sophocles. The greatest moment of his career was his appearance as Oedipus in Reinhardt's production at Covent Garden for three weeks in 1912. Though the play had been used as a text-book by several generations of schoolboys, it was banned by the censor for public performance, and it took some time to convince him that what was considered safe for schoolboys in Greek could not be very dangerous for adults in English. The translation was by Gilbert Murray, and Harvey was the first person to act the part in England since Betterton played it over two centuries before. The production was the sensation of the day; Harvey was magnificent in the chief part; and the Opera House was packed at every performance.

Yet he never made much money in London and had to depend on the provinces and Canada for his livelihood. Take the example of what was on the whole his most interesting Shakespearean production, *The Taming of the Shrew*, in which

Martin-Harvey in
The Corsican Brothers

Martin-Harvey in
A Cigarette Maker's Romance

Martin-Harvey
as Boy O'Carroll

Martin-Harvey as Pelléas
in Maeterlinck's play

H. B. Irving in *The Bells*

H. B. Irving as Charles I   H. B. Irving as Markheim

Lewis Waller and H. B. Irving
as Othello and Iago

H. B. Irving and Dorothea Baird
in *Louis XI*

H. B. Irving as Hyde, and Eille Norwood,
in *Dr. Jekyll and Mr. Hyde* by R. L. Stevenson

H. B. Irving and Irene Vanbrugh
in *The Admirable Crichton*
by James Barrie

H. B. Irving as Wogan
in *Princess Clementina*
by A. E. W. Mason

Scene from H. B. Irving's production of *The Lyons Mail*

he reacted against the elaborate realism of Tree's presentations by staging it simply, effectively, and inexpensively; reacted also against the common portrayal of Petruchio as a bully by playing him as a gentleman enjoying a frolic, his method of courtship nothing but a good-natured joke. It was an entirely charming entertainment; but the average nightly receipts in London were £41, whereas in Edinburgh they had been £152. One of the reasons why Londoners did not flock to see him was that his wife's acting, to put it mildly, was not as good as his; but he always cast her for a part because he thought it was. He never forgot that *The Only Way* was due to her, and his devotion no less than his gratitude made him over-estimate her ability as an actress. But perhaps the chief reason that he never became a West End favourite was that the type of play he did, which called for his type of acting, was going out of fashion. Melodramas and broad histrionic effects were becoming things of the past. Even Sir Henry Irving was losing popularity in the last decade of his life. Harvey would now be called a 'ham' actor by all those who confuse the underacting of today with natural acting. As a matter of fact he was perfectly adapted to the class of play he produced, and if *The Only Way* or *The Breed of the Treshams* were staged at the present time they would be utterly ineffective because no modern actor could put them over. It is well to remember that both Shakespeare and Shaw wrote their plays for 'ham' actors; that is to say, for men who knew how to deliver a long speech with the rhetorical flourish necessary to maintain interest and the vocal control to build up the climax.

One example of Harvey's acting made me laugh, another made me hold my breath, but even the one that amused me showed the right method in that particular play. It was *The Corsican Brothers*, a stage version of Alexandre Dumas's novel, which Harvey revived at the Adelphi Theatre in 1907. In the last act the hero, who in his dual capacity has been monopolising the interest throughout, stamps up and down the stage threatening vengeance on the villain who has killed his brother. 'Am I your brother's keeper?' asks the villain sardonically. 'The answer of the first murderer!' exclaims the hero passionately, again declaring his firm intention to slay the slayer and revenge his brother. At this point the villain, an expert swordsman, calls the hero a 'pitiful boaster'; upon which the hero, slap in the centre of the stage, the focus of all the limelight, stares about him with incredulous amazement and with a shattered howl demands: 'Gentlemen, do I *look* like a booaaster?' It was not Harvey's fault if he didn't. On the occasion when I held my breath, the rest of the audience were in a similar plight. It was when Harvey in *The Breed of the Treshams* tells the story of his somewhat disreputable life. The words are commonplace enough, but his manner of speaking them was so masterly that there was not a cough or a movement from the crowded house at the Lyceum; and when, in the middle of his tale, he broke his clay pipe, the sound of the snap went through the audience like an electric shock, and their quick intake of breath was like an involuntary gasp of relief.

Harvey's unique gift as an actor was his power to create atmosphere. By merely looking over his shoulder he could make you feel that something sinister was behind him; by a simple movement of his hands he could suggest tension; by an inflection of his voice he could generate fear or sympathy or sorrow or romance or any emotion connected with romance. For this reason his Hamlet, Richard III and Henry V were a little disappointing. They were good, but not as good as one had expected them to be. He put too much mystery and not enough heroism into them. And he could not impersonate a perfectly ordinary human being, one who behaved in a practical common-sense manner. He failed to comprehend Dick Dudgeon, the part he played in *The Devil's Disciple*, because Dick's sacrifice was entirely unromantic; and he begged Shaw to rewrite parts of the drama, as the audiences were confused and he was losing money. Shaw replied that he ought to be in the workhouse; which no doubt he would have been had he continued to play Shaw, whom he could not understand, instead of Dickens, whom he could.

His last appearance on the stage as actor and manager was at Newcastle-on-Tyne in May 1939, when at the age of seventy-six he played the part of Sydney Carton, a performance that had fascinated playgoers for forty years.

H. B. IRVING
(1870–1919)

THERE are great advantages and grave disadvantages in being the son of a famous father. If the son adopts a different profession from the father, the advantages prevail; if he follows the same profession, the comparison between the two is never in his favour. H. B. Irving, known in the theatre world of his time as Harry Irving, would perhaps have been wise to become a barrister instead of an actor. He was educated for the law, and his father, Sir Henry Irving, whose reputation at his death in 1905 has only been paralleled in theatrical history by that of David Garrick, did his best to discourage both his boys, Harry and Laurence, from following in his footsteps. But Harry became a keen amateur actor while still at Oxford, and his performances of Shakespeare's King John and Browning's Strafford for the O.U.D.S. created much interest. The moment he left the University in 1891 his father's friend John Hare engaged him to play at the Garrick Theatre, but he made little impression and once more turned his attention to the law, incidentally working on a Life of Judge Jeffreys, in which he contrived to make a hero of that super-criminal. He was called to the Bar by the Inner Temple in 1894, and in the same year reappeared on the stage under the management of another of his father's friends. Again his amateurishness was too apparent, and he determined to gain experience in the provinces, joining the Shakespearean company of Ben Greet, and, because he was the son of his father, playing a number of important parts instead of learning his job properly by starting at the bottom.

It was scarcely surprising that his father should have viewed his progress with a sardonic eye. Ben Webster told me that at rehearsals one day in 1895, wishing to ingratiate himself with Henry Irving, he said how pleased he was to see in the papers that Harry would shortly appear in the provinces as Hamlet. No sign of pleasure appeared on the face of the father, who grunted: 'Harr-y . . . hm . . . Ham-let . . . Hm . . . Sill-y . . .' When, ten years later, Harry played Hamlet in Oscar Asche's production at the Adelphi Theatre, London, his father was present on the first night. Afterwards there was a supper-party at Romano's, throughout which Harry was in a state of suppressed agitation because the great man had said nothing about his performance. At three in the morning Henry Irving got up to go home; a hansom cab was called; and Harry accompanied his father to the street. Still not a syllable about his Hamlet had been uttered. Then, just as the cab began to move, his father leant forward and said: 'Well, good night, me boy . . . Hm . . . D'ye like yer part?'

This was rather cruel, but Harry could be sardonic enough at his father's expense. The following was told me by Bernard Shaw, whose criticism of Sir Henry Irving's revival of *Richard III* caused a sensation: 'I wrote a faithful but extremely stupid notice of the performance, in which I said that he did not seem to be "answering his helm" as usual. I call this stupid because I ought to have seen that what was the matter was that he had drunk a little too much: an explanation which had not occurred to me. Irving, unfortunately, did not believe that I was so innocent, and regarded my criticism as a veiled and malicious accusation of drunkenness. . . . I happened to meet Frederick Harrison, manager of the Haymarket Theatre, who, to my astonishment, spoke of the appalling crime I had committed and the terrible commotion at the Lyceum Theatre about it. At first I was incredulous, and asked him who had told him all this. He said he had just had it from Harry Irving, whose characteristically Irving-esque comment was that it served the old man right and would teach him to keep sober next time.'

In July 1896 Harry Irving married Dorothea Baird, who had recently played Trilby in Tree's production, and a month later he joined the company at the St James's Theatre, remaining with George Alexander for five years, and learning his job thoroughly for the first time. What brought him to the front was his performance of the name-part in Barrie's *The Admirable Crichton* (1902). Many people considered that he never again acted so well. He certainly did not act well in the revival of another comedy by Barrie, *The Professor's Love Story.* 'You're like nothing on earth', was the criticism of an old friend. 'In that case', replied Harry, 'I must be like something in Barrie.'

His first appearance as Hamlet in the West End was in 1905, and the following year he played Iago to Lewis Waller's Othello. Then he formed a company of his own and revived several of his father's old melodramas, making a big success both in London and on tour with *The Lyons Mail*, but not doing so well with *Charles I, Louis XI* and *The Bells.* I saw him in all these plays; and though he was extremely enter-taining as Dubosc in the first and comically grotesque as Louis XI, I never for a moment forgot that I was in a theatre witnessing a histrionic exhibition. His Brewster in *A Story of Waterloo*, another part made famous by his father, was a preposterous caricature of senility. As for his Hamlet, I could scarcely believe my ears when first I sat through it, so went again in the hope that they had deceived me. They had not. He had no notion of the music of the verse, which he delivered in a drawling and meaningless monotone. For a Shakespeare-lover it was a most distressing experience; and if his name had not been Irving the critics might not have been so polite, though the boredom they endure in the exercise of their profession trains them to suffer almost anything.

The worst of the actor-manager system was that it too often gorged the vanity of the leading actor until the size of his head was out of all proportion to the rest of his body. He became the little god of his theatre, and the other performers were there merely to reflect his glory. A friend of mine once played the King to Harry Irving's Hamlet, and told me that the King's opening speech was accompanied by a series of *sotto voce* commands from Hamlet to hurry up. While the wretched monarch was speaking of 'our sometime sister, now our queen, the imperial jointress to this warlike state', etc., the supposedly silent Hamlet was muttering 'Get on with it . . . they aren't listening . . . no one's interested . . . quicker, quicker . . . cut it short.' If I had been playing the King I would have stopped dead and quietly suggested to Hamlet that he could get on with it. But my friend did not wish to be sacked, and finished the speech at a rate that may have placated Irving but cannot have clarified Shakespeare.

Harry Irving's best Shakespearean performance was his Iago. With his white face, his long black hair, his cynical expression, and his intense interest in crime and criminals, he seemed fitted to play parts of a sinister nature, and he became notable as an actor of stage-villains; but he was more attractive as a light comedian. The best performance I ever saw him give was in a farcical comedy called *The Angel in the House* by Eden Phillpotts and Basil Macdonald Hastings; and when he announced his intention to present a dramatic version of Oscar Wilde's story 'Lord Arthur Savile's Crime' I felt sure that it was just the thing for him, as a satirical theme spiced with crime would have suited his style to a nicety; but he did not produce it. I was present in his dressing-room at the Savoy Theatre, of which he became lessee and manager in 1913, when he told the tale as he had originally heard it from Wilde. After he had finished, someone said:

'Very good, as a sketch. But one doesn't want three acts of it.'

'I agree', nodded Irving.

'Then you don't intend to do it?'

'Not in three acts.'

'In one, then, as a curtain-raiser?'

'No, in four.' When our laughter had subsided, he added thoughtfully: 'And a prologue.'

Hamlet apart, the only poetic play he produced while in management was *The Sin of David* by Stephen Phillips. Because of his obsession with crime, he was much too fond of doing pathological studies of the Stevensonian kind, such as *Markheim*, *Jekyll and Hyde*. He was one of the enthusiasts who founded The Crimes Club, and he never missed their dinners if he could help it. He was a frequent visitor at the Old Bailey during the trials of notorious criminals. And he wrote three or four books dealing with eminent murderers and burglars. This morbid interest in moronic complaints proves that he never outgrew his adolescence, and explains his inability to perceive where his real strength as an actor lay. I would have cast him without hesitation for the part of John Worthing in *The Importance of Being Earnest*, and his brother Laurence, who usually played lugubrious parts, for Algy in the same play.

Though both of them were famous in their day, neither appears to have impressed the editor of *The Dictionary of National Biography*. In one of his biographical studies, Harry Irving complains that 'the greatest and most naturally gifted criminal England has produced', Charles Peace, is omitted from that compilation, which includes many less remarkable law-breakers. The same fate has overtaken the Irving brothers, for both of whom space should have been found in the 1912–21 volume between the not more notable names of Elsie Maud Inglis, physician and surgeon, and Henry Jackson, Regius Professor of Greek at Cambridge.

LAURENCE IRVING
(1871–1914)

IF the elder brother's career was shadowed by his father's, the younger's start in life would not have been helped by two family reputations in the same profession at the same time, especially as he felt no desire to compete with them. Laurence Irving wished to enter the Diplomatic Service, and went to Russia with an introduction to the English Ambassador at St Petersburg, where he spent three years, learning the language and steeping himself in Russian literature. Unfortunately, when the moment came for him to enter the Service, his father could not afford to maintain him in the early stages of his vocation; which was perhaps as well, for Laurence had too explosive a nature and too much sympathy with the underdog to succeed in diplomacy.

There was nothing for it but to go on the stage, and at the age of twenty he joined the Benson Company, which he left because of an accident with a pistol, the bullet of which just missed his heart. The rumour, prevalent in his profession, that he had attempted suicide, was due to his unhappiness in the company: he disliked games, he did not think practical jokes funny, he was not amused by leg-pulling, and he took his work very seriously. After an engagement in the company of his father's old friend J. L. Toole, and a tour of *Trilby* in which he played Svengali, he joined his father at the Lyceum Theatre, where he acted several parts and in his spare time wrote several plays, one of which, *Peter the Great*, was produced by his father; but though the leading parts were played by Sir Henry and Ellen Terry, it was a failure. He also translated Sardou's *Robespierre*, which was staged by his father in 1899.

Ten years later Laurence presented his translations of two plays by Brieux in America, where he got into hot water with the dramatic critics by describing *The Merry Widow* as 'a highly deleterious entertainment', which was roughly how the critics were describing the plays of Brieux. On returning to England in 1910 he did his own version of Dostoievsky's *Crime and Punishment*, which he called *The Unwritten Law*. This, together with a play on Margaret Catchpole and a drama of French life called *The Lily*, though none of them was successful, established him in management; and thereafter he and his wife Mabel Hackney were recognised as leading figures on the London and provincial stage. In 1911 he played *Hamlet* in the provinces, dressing it in the period of Queen Elizabeth. His was a high-spirited, humorous, brainy Prince, who, because he had little feeling for verse, could not realise Shakespeare's conception.

Laurence was an uneven actor, either very good or very bad. Ellen Terry thought him excellent as Captain Brassbound in Shaw's comedy. She had tried to induce Sir Henry Irving to produce this play, with what result Shaw told me: 'He put his finger on the scene where Brassbound comes in in a frock coat and top hat, and said "Shaw put that in to get me laughed at." He was perfectly right; and the stroke was so successful that when Laurence Irving created the part the audience laughed for two solid minutes at him at this point.'

The boyishness and good-nature of Laurence appealed strongly to Ellen Terry, who much preferred him to his brother. 'H.B. is so modern, slangy of speech it seems to me', she wrote to Shaw; 'and oh, how old he is compared with *my* Irving boy.'

Laurence played Iago to Tree's Othello in 1912, and I found the comparison between his conception of the part and his brother's illuminating. Harry saw Iago as a subtle,

urence Irving and Mabel Hackney
in *The Unwritten Law*

Scene from Laurence Irving's
production of *The Lily*

Laurence Irving and Mabel Hackney in *Typhoon*

Asche as Falstaff, and Roy Royston as Robin, in *The Merry Wives of Winds*

Scene from Asche's production of *The Merry Wives of Windsor*

Oscar Asche as Chu-Chin-Chow

Asche as Christopher Sly
in the Induction to
The Taming of the Shrew

Asche as Petruchio
in *The Taming of the Shrew*

Asche and Lily Brayton in *Kismet*

machiavellian villain, revelling in his devilment and relishing his power. Laurence saw him as a bluff soldier, who has become jealous, resentful, and malignant. The first was the more entertaining, the second the more intelligent. Laurence was fond of the didactic drama, admired Ibsen, Shaw, and Tolstoy, and would probably have founded something in the nature of a repertory theatre, mainly devoted to sombre pieces, if his life had not been cut short. His performance of Earl Skule in Ibsen's *The Pretenders*, which he produced in 1913 at the Haymarket Theatre, made me feel that he had been born to act Macbeth if only he could have learnt to speak Shakespeare's lines as poetry instead of prose.

After years of struggling against the public apathy towards plays with a purpose, he quite unexpectedly scored a success in his own adaptation of a Hungarian drama of Japanese life, called *Typhoon*, in which he seemed to be more oriental than the real Japanese members of the cast. It ran for over 200 performances at four London theatres. A profitable tour of Canada followed early in 1914; but on their way home his wife and himself were drowned when *The Empress of Ireland* was rammed by a Norwegian collier in a dense fog, and sank in ten minutes.

OSCAR ASCHE
(1871–1936)

AN Australian by birth, Oscar Asche spent his youth in surroundings that were not conducive to the study of poetry. His father was a Norwegian who spoke broken English and who had been a policeman, a gold-digger, a land agent, a storekeeper, and a publican. Oscar's upbringing was a pretty rough-and-tumble affair. As a young man he ran away from home and lived for months alone in the bush, killing and cooking his own food, reading Shakespeare aloud to a greyhound, and hoping that some day he would act in the plays of one and enter the other for races. After many escapades his father sent him to Norway to learn acting, and his culinary skill was immediately useful on the boat, because the cook deserted just before they left port, and the passengers as well as the crew had to depend on Asche for everything they ate except biscuits and tinned fruit. He could kill, skin and clean a sheep in five minutes, and his only failure was in the sweets department, several passengers remaining in their cabins for some time after he had served up a boiled currant pudding.

Having spent a few months in Norway studying acting and elocution, he arrived in England and obtained an interview with F. R. Benson, who closely questioned him about cricket and engaged him at once on his assurance that he was a first-rate wicket-keeper. Asche was a brawny fellow, and Benson promptly revived *As You Like It* for the express purpose of giving him the part of Charles and enjoying a strenuous wrestling match with him in Act I. This was in 1893. But Asche was getting no money from home, and when the Benson Company were out of work in the summer months he had to sleep on the Thames embankment and earn occasional pennies by calling cabs for rich playgoers after the evening performances. He found the loneliness of London far more trying than the loneliness of the Australian bush.

After eight years with Benson, during which he worked his way up from insignificant 'messengers' to second 'leads', he joined Tree at His Majesty's, where he acted important parts and helped to produce several plays. Another Old Bensonian named Otho Stuart took the Adelphi Theatre in 1904, put up the necessary money, and asked Asche to join him. Their second production was *The Taming of the Shrew*, in which Asche doubled the parts of Christopher Sly and Petruchio, his wife Lily Brayton was incomparably the best Katharina of her time, and both of them jumped at a bound to the front of their profession. It was a breathless, knockabout, rampageous show, played on broadly farcical lines, and the audiences rocked with laughter. Wherever performed it raised the roof, and Oscar Asche and Lily Brayton played it some fifteen hundred times in the United Kingdom and elsewhere. It was followed at the Adelphi by *Hamlet*, with H. B. Irving in the leading part, Oscar Asche as Claudius and Lily Brayton as Ophelia; and this was followed by *Measure for Measure* and *A Midsummer Night's Dream*. They also did a blank verse play by Rudolf Besier called *The Virgin Goddess*, which was received with wild enthusiasm by the first-night audience, acclaimed as a masterpiece by the critics, and ran for five weeks at a dead loss.

Following three years of worthy endeavour at the Adelphi, Asche produced *Othello* on tour. He had immense vocal and physical power and made an alarming figure of the Moor. The big scene in the third act was a tempestuous business; he shook Iago as a terrier shakes a rat; haled him up and down the stage, dashed him to the ground, half-throttled him, and forced one to wonder whether the actor who played the part demanded double his normal salary and the nightly presence of a doctor in the wings.

Two philanthropists wanted Asche for the part of Attila in a poetic play by Laurence Binyon. He agreed to play it if there was enough money to follow it with *As You Like It*. Apparently there was, and he produced the first at His Majesty's Theatre while Tree was in the provinces. It failed, as he thought it would, but *As You Like It* (1907) with Henry Ainley as Orlando, Lily Brayton as Rosalind, Godfrey Tearle as Silvius, Courtice Pounds as Touchstone, and Asche himself as Jaques, was a success. In staging the Forest of Arden scenes Asche out-Beerbohmed Tree. Few real forest glades could compete with his artificial ones: there were masses of ferns two feet high, trodden down by the characters and renewed weekly; the ground was covered thick with autumn leaves; fallen logs were half-hidden by moss; clumps of bamboo grew among the trees; Rosalind emerged from a straw-thatched cottage; rows of pines disappeared into the glimmering distance; and to complete the illusion of rusticity Asche ate an apple while delivering the Seven Ages speech.

A year or two later he perplexed the critics by putting on *The Merry Wives of Windsor* in a Christmas-card setting, the characters being well wrapped up, breathing on their fingers, flapping their arms, and shuffling quickly through four inches of salty snow. Then he moved to the tropics, and in 1911 produced a play by Edward Knoblock which had been hawked round London and New York without impressing a single manager. Much to the annoyance of the author, Asche cut chunks out of the dialogue, introduced new scenes, renamed it *Kismet*, and played Hajj the beggar quite differently from the part as written; but, less to the author's annoyance, he made a huge success of it, the gorgeous oriental scenery and dresses drawing all playgoing London.

After that Asche tended to judge a play by its scenic possibilities, and in a drama he staged on Zulu life called *Mameena* the costumes and properties were fashioned in the kraals of Zulus, who had to hunt and kill wild animals for their hide and fur, to make assagais and knobkerries, and to slay forty oxen in order to provide eighty war-shields. For this show Asche instituted a system of lighting which was copied in Germany, reintroduced to England some ten years later, and acclaimed in the press as a wonderful German invention. All the characters in *Mameena* with one exception were brown or black, and it took them two hours to colour themselves from head to foot. But in spite of the efforts of the producer, the pains of the cast, the thrilling Zulu war-dance, and the phenomenal cost, the thing was a failure, possibly because of the street-lighting restrictions which were enforced towards the close of 1914.

Asche was a very good all-round actor; what sinews and lung-power could do, he did; but lacking subtlety he never gave a great performance. His Othello was as good as his Petruchio, his Sly as his Angelo, his Hannibal as his Hajj; but not one of them was notably brilliant in execution or original in conception. 'If I had Forbes-Robertson's face I'd be the most famous actor in the world', he once half-jokingly declared. The fellow to whom this was said would have liked to reply 'You could also do with Forbes-Robertson's sensitiveness, voice, charm, and one or two other things'; but as he did not wish to be tossed out of the window or to come violently into contact with the ceiling, he refrained. Asche had an excellent voice, though its quality was hard and slightly metallic, and every syllable he uttered could be heard in the farthest corner of the largest theatre in the kingdom. He could be tender, but his expression of the softer emotions was a little disturbing, like a giant weeping (not that I've ever seen a

68

weeping giant), and seemed rather out of character. Personally, he was a pleasant, jovial fellow, who liked practical jokes, loved cricket, played games as well as he played parts, enjoyed good food, and was a first-class cook, quite capable of preparing a five-course meal for a dozen people at the side of the road when out motoring. Also he was by no means a negligible writer. He dramatised that excellent romance *Count Hannibal* by Stanley Weyman, and made a success of it; he cut *Kismet* to bits, pulled it together, and scored a bull's eye; he wrote the raciest and most honest book of purely theatrical reminiscences I have ever come across; and he did the lyrics as well as the dialogue of two musical shows, one of which had the record run of any piece in the history of the stage: *Chu-Chin-Chow*.

The first half of this work was dictated at Manchester because it was raining and he could not play golf, the second half at Glasgow because he was alone and had nothing else to do. It was financed in equal shares by Beerbohm Tree, who was away in America, and by Lily Brayton. The music was composed by Frederick Norton, and the show was produced by Asche at His Majesty's Theatre on August 31st, 1916, running until July 22nd, 1921, a total of 2,235 performances. Everyone concerned with its production made a fortune, and Asche himself drew well over £200,000 in royalties. The boredom of playing the same part for close on five years permanently harmed him as an actor, though he missed performances when not in the mood. Hubert Carter, who understudied him, told me that Asche's presence in the theatre at night was no guarantee that he would be playing. One evening he walked up to his dressing-room, started to change, suddenly said to his dresser 'Don't think I'll go on tonight', and went back to his club, leaving Carter about ten minutes to dress, make-up, and appear as Chu Chin Chow. The fabulous success of the show also ruined him financially.

He threw his money to the dogs. The farm he took in the Cotswolds, where at one time he had seventy-two greyhounds in his kennels, resulted in a heavy loss. Something like £100,000 disappeared in this way, and he reckoned that he had spent about £45,000 on his dogs apart from what he had lost in backing them at races. He lived right up to his income; and as this enabled him to live extremely well, he became fat enough to play Falstaff without padding.

Chu-Chin-Chow was followed by his musical play *Cairo*, the most elaborate production that has ever appeared on the English stage. It made a handsome profit; but the reaction against these dazzling spectacles had begun to set in, and Asche went off to Australia for the third time, adding *Julius Caesar*, *Antony and Cleopatra* and *The Merchant of Venice* to his repertory. When he started rehearsing *Julius Caesar*, he had no copies of the play; so he got a stenographer and dictated the version in which he had last appeared some ten years previously. Later it was found that he had scarcely made a dozen mistakes in the text. All his tours in his native continent were enormously successful; Australia was proud of her son; and wherever he went there were banquets and municipal receptions in his honour.

His last notable production in London was *Julius Caesar* at His Majesty's, when Godfrey Tearle gave the best performance of Antony I have seen and Lyn Harding gave the only intelligent performance of Julius Caesar I can remember, but Asche as Casca showed little of his early resilience.

Until he won a fortune and lost his figure with *Chu-Chin-Chow*, his work for the stage had been admirable. More than anyone else he carried on the Bensonian tradition of combining Shakespeare with sport, and the costliness of his productions and his private extravagance were matched by his generosity to his fellow-artists.

Scene from Asche's production of *Mameena*

Asche and Lily Brayton in *Count Hannibal*

CONTRAST

Lily Brayton and Oscar Asche in *Measure for Measure*

Asche as Bottom (second from left)
in his production of *A Midsummer Night's Dream*

HARLEY GRANVILLE-BARKER
(1877-1946)

NOWADAYS Granville-Barker is remembered chiefly as a producer, and few people seem to know that he was both an actor and a manager. Yet it is no exaggeration to say that his seasons at the Court Theatre from 1904 to 1907 were the most important events in the history of the British stage since Shakespeare and Burbage ran the Globe Theatre on Bankside; for during those three years Bernard Shaw made his English reputation as a dramatist, his plays being produced by himself with Barker in the leading parts.

Many remarkable men are found to be mongrels if their pedigrees are traced back for three generations, and in Barker's case his great-grandfather was an Italian-born physician named Bozzi who, when he settled in England, took the surname of his maternal grandmother Rosa Granville. Barker's father was an architect turned building speculator, and cannot have been doing well during the minority of Harley, who had to leave home and go on the stage at the age of fourteen. After a preliminary canter in a London musical piece, he joined Ben Greet's Shakespearean company on tour, and at the age of twenty was cast by William Poel for the part of Shakespeare's Richard II in a production by the Elizabethan Stage Society. Five years later he played Marlowe's Edward II for the same society at Oxford, and these two performances founded his fame as an actor, while Poel's methods influenced his own when he became a Shakespearean producer. The formation of the Stage Society in 1899, and his acting at their Sunday night and Monday afternoon performances for members, brought him to the notice of those who were promoting the new drama of ideas. At that time Shaw's *Candida* was about to be done by the Stage Society, and 'I was at my wit's end for an actor who could do justice to the part of Marchbanks', said Shaw to me, 'when one day I dropped in to a matinée of Hauptmann's *Friedenfest*, and instantly saw the very fellow for my poet. I wrote to announce my wonderful discovery to Janet Achurch and her husband, who had been touring *Candida* in the provinces, and they replied that they had frequently mentioned Barker to me as the ideal man for the part.' That was the beginning of the great Shaw-Barker combination. *Candida* was played for two performances in July 1900, and Barker was as perfect in his part as a human being could be.

In 1904 a series of Shakespearean revivals were being given by an enthusiast named J. H. Leigh at the Court Theatre. His manager, J. E. Vedrenne, asked Barker to superintend *Two Gentlemen of Verona*. Barker was willing on condition that Vedrenne would join him in presenting half a dozen matinées of *Candida*. Vedrenne agreed; the matinées were successful; the partners joined forces; and the Vedrenne-Barker management commenced operations at the Court in the autumn of 1904. Starting with matinées, they were soon able to give evening performances as well, because Shaw's new play *John Bull's Other Island* (November 1904) with Barker as Father Keegan was an instantaneous success. It was followed by *Man and Superman* (May 1905) with Barker as Tanner, *Major Barbara* (November 1905) in which Barker imitated Gilbert Murray (the original) as Cusins, *Captain Brassbound's Conversion* (March 1906) with Ellen Terry in the part written for her and Frederick Kerr as Brassbound, and *The Doctor's Dilemma* (November 1906) with Barker as Dubedat. Shaw's earlier plays were also revived, Barker playing Valentine in the most popular of these, *You Never Can Tell*. It was the

commencement of the repertory movement in London, each
new play being performed for a few weeks, taken off for
another play, and revived again at intervals. Shaw was the
producer of all his own comedies, while Barker was responsible for the rest, including works by himself, by Ibsen,
Maeterlinck, Galsworthy, Masefield, St John Hankin, and the
translations by Gilbert Murray of *Hippolytus*, *The Trojan Women*
and *The Electra* of Euripides. Shaw considered that Barker's
productions of these last three were the highest achievement
of his management. Others would say that Shaw's productions of his own plays were the great events of the Vedrenne-
Barker partnership; and indeed everything else was made
possible by the Shavian successes, which financed the firm.

As an actor Barker was poetic, subtle, and low-toned.
Being completely unathletic, he tended always to underplay
his parts; for he grew up in the nervous modern school of
Irving and Duse, which was very effective in such characters
as Keegan, Marchbanks, Cusins and Dubedat, but was too
quiet for Tanner, Valentine, Burgoyne (in which he failed)
and Saranoff. Shaw's long speeches, like Shakespeare's, call
for the majesty and flamboyance of Barry Sullivan, Salvini
and Ristori, by whom Shaw was stage-struck in his boyhood,
and whom Barker had never seen. Barker's gentle manner, together with something adenoidal in his delivery, prevented him
from doing justice to the more superhuman Shavian heroes.
'He is always useful when a touch of poetry and refinement
is needed', said Shaw: 'he lifts a whole cast when his part gives
him a chance, even when he lets the part down and makes the
author swear. He rebukes me feelingly for wanting my parts
to be "caricatured".' Barker was greatly helped throughout
his stage career by his wife, Lillah McCarthy, who made a
Siddonian Shavian heroine and scored personal triumphs in
Masefield's *Nan* and a gloomy play called *The Witch*.

As a man Barker was extremely wilful and opinionated. When he wanted to do a thing, he did it. When he made up his mind, nothing could change it. He was indifferent to people's feelings where his own were involved. Shaw summed him up as 'a cold-hearted Italian devil, but a noble soul all the same'. He was a curious combination of ruthlessness, charm, high-mindedness, and sociability. He had read widely, knew Shakespeare and Dickens almost by heart, and had formed a prose style of his own that was precious and pedantic. His plays were interesting but rather lifeless: the themes were vital, but the treatment lacked zest. One of them, *Waste*, was refused a licence by the Lord Chamberlain, and some passages of the evidence given by Barker on the censorship before a parliamentary committee throw light on his character:

'He (the censor) wrote to me and demanded first of all general alterations. I asked him to specify them. He said in a letter that it was not necessary to indicate particular lines, but I must be prepared to moderate and modify the extremely outspoken references to sexual relations. . . . I replied that I considered in such a play sober, plain speaking to be the only honest course; that innuendo would be indecent, and that while I naturally could not admit that I had written anything unfit to be spoken in the theatre, and it was difficult to delegate my responsibility in such delicate matters to him, still, if he would name the particular phrases which he objected to, I would consider their alteration. To that he paid no attention whatever. You see that it was clearly impossible for me to reply to a vague accusation, because it would have been admitting that I had written something of which I was ashamed, which I considered was indecent—and that an author cannot do. . . . He further demanded that I should eliminate entirely all reference to a criminal operation. Now I myself produced at the Court Theatre a few months before,

Bernard Shaw and Granville-Barker
(c. 1900)

Ellen Terry and Fred Kerr
in *Captain Brassbound's Conversion*
by Bernard Shaw

Granville-Barker, Fanny Brough, and Charles Goodhart
in a scene from Shaw's *Mrs. Warren's Profession* (1902)

The Forum Scene in Tree's production of *Julius Caes*
(Tree as Antony is star

nation Gala Performance at His Majesty's Theatre, 1911
 his back to the rostrum)

Scene from Granville-Barker's production of Shaw's *Androcles and the Lion* (1913)
(left to right)—Ben Webster as the Captain; Lillah McCarthy as Lavinia;
Baliol Holloway as the Menagerie Keeper; Leon Quartermaine as the Emperor;
Edward Sillward as the Lion; O. P. Heggie as Androcles; Alfred Brydone as
Ferrovius; Herbert Hewetson as the Editor

Scene from Granville-Barker's production of *The Winter's Tale* (1912)
(left to right)—Stanley Drewitt as Camillo; Cathleen Nesbitt as Perdita;
H. O. Nicholson as the Old Shepherd; Dennis Neilson-Terry as Florizel

under the Lord Chamberlain's licence, a play, the plot of which partly turned upon a criminal operation which was quite openly referred to on the stage. Therefore, in writing *Waste*, I could not possibly be supposed to know that the reference to this subject would be made a definite reason for refusing to licence the play. . . .'

Asked whether it was much of a shock to him when *Waste* was refused a licence, Barker replied that it was a great disappointment. 'But you were not altogether surprised?' 'I am never surprised at the action of the Lord Chamberlain.'

As a producer of modern plays of the intimate, realistic school, such as his own and Galsworthy's, there was no one to touch Barker, and he has had no comparable successor. He tried to make actors conceive their parts, instead of just learning them and making them theatrically effective. To do this he would take an actor aside and sketch the life-history of the character he was studying, even going so far as to mention the character's habits and hobbies, thoughts and tastes, whether he took salt or sugar with his porridge, why he preferred Tennyson to Shakespeare, and so on, all with the object of forcing the actor to think himself into a character, to live it as a whole, not speak it as a part, to earn a place in the story, not shine as a 'star' on the stage. Of course the players could make nothing of all this; yet Barker managed to create something that had not been seen in the theatre before his time; he really did make his actors give forth some quality of which they had previously been unaware; and the result was that the plays he presented had a lifelike atmosphere about them which gave an audience the feeling that they were sharing in the drama, not merely watching it as spectators.

But when Barker tackled Shakespeare and Shaw he broke down. Those two dramatists demand colour, sound, movement, the flourish of rhetoric, everything in fact that does not

in the least resemble the humdrum life of the suburbs; and
though Barker brought off some exquisite moments in the
quieter and more lyrical passages of Shakespeare, the plays
as a whole evaded him. As Shaw said, he hated acting, and
managed to get something else. I recall an amusing episode
when his instructions were swept aside without a word of
explanation or excuse by Tree, who was acting Antony in the
Forum scene from *Julius Caesar* at the Coronation Gala Performance in 1911. Barker, having by then achieved considerable prestige in the theatrical world, was asked to
produce the scene. The crowd consisted of some three
hundred actors, well-known and unknown, who packed the
arcade behind His Majesty's Theatre when they used it as a
dressing-room for the performance. Barker had gone to great
trouble to prepare a pamphlet of some twenty-four pages in
which the movements of every member of the mob were
carefully noted at each stage of the proceedings: e.g. 'X 186
groans heavily and moves up stage, where he joins a doleful
group consisting of Ys 48–54 and Zs 201–10', or something of
that sort. It was a remarkable effort and must have cost
Barker many weary hours of thought; but he had overlooked
the simple fact that it would have taken about two months'
hard rehearsing to get the effect at which he aimed. His
early frantic attempts, with the aid of a powerful bell, to
control the crowd of 'stars', 'semi-stars' and 'walking gentlemen', were about as successful as would be an attempt to
secure order in a monkey-house into which a few elephants,
tigers, peacocks and parrots had strayed. After two or three
desperate and chaotic rehearsals, Tree came on the scene.
Barker's pamphlets were promptly scrapped, and Tree's
simple method was adopted of letting the rabble do what they
liked when given free rein, while attending in dead silence
to Antony whenever he was orating.

Had Barker remained at the Court Theatre, assured of all the success possible with domestic plays at an intimate playhouse, he would have justified the existence of repertory in the West End; but, like Bolingbroke in *Richard II*, his resolution soared to a higher pitch. Towards the close of 1907 the Vedrenne-Barker management moved to the Savoy, where they added *Caesar and Cleopatra* (with Forbes-Robertson), *The Devil's Disciple* and *Arms and The Man* to the Shavian cycle, and also took the Haymarket Theatre for a new Shaw play, *Getting Married*. The management were soon in debt and had to close down. Vedrenne, an ex-consul who had no capital and no cultural enthusiasms, was penniless. Shaw and Barker had to foot the bill. 'Barker had to pawn his clothes, and I disgorged most of my royalties', Shaw informed me; 'but the creditors were paid in full.'

J. M. Barrie then persuaded Charles Frohman, an American manager who controlled the Duke of York's Theatre, to try highbrow repertory there in 1910. Frohman, convinced that under his direction even highbrow stuff would succeed, witnessed with growing dismay Barker's *The Madras House*, Galsworthy's *Justice*, a comedy by Meredith, a playlet by Barrie about a child heroine who was an incurable dipsomaniac, and Shaw's *Misalliance*, all playing to about £100 a night instead of the £300 which he regarded as his minimum. When a revival of Pinero's *Trelawny of the Wells* sent the receipts sky high, he threw repertory to the winds, leaving Barker convinced that only in a municipal theatre rent, and rate free, could repertory pay its way.

Next Barker got Lord Howard de Walden to finance seasons at the Little Theatre in 1911 (*Fanny's First Play*), at the St James's in 1913 (*Androcles and The Lion*, followed by repertory), and at the Savoy, where he staged three of Shakespeare's comedies: *The Winter's Tale*, *Twelfth Night* and

A Midsummer Night's Dream. These productions made a sensation. Their great merit was that the plays were performed in their entirety word for word as Shakespeare had written them, which meant that the actors had to speak a great deal faster than the pace to which they were accustomed. Their chief fault was that too often the beauty of the verse was sacrificed to speed and naturalism. The scenery and costumes had a new beauty; for Barker's taste was exquisite; but his dislike of Shakespearean acting led him to some undercasting and underplaying. Still, it was a notable enterprise, and made an end of the practice of cutting the plays to shreds to gratify the egotism and vanity of 'star' players and provide long intervals for the profit of the refreshment bars.

After staging his own arrangement of scenes from Thomas Hardy's *The Dynasts*, Barker went to America at the end of 1914 to produce *Androcles and The Lion* and to consider an offer to direct the Millionaires Theatre in New York. This he declined on finding that the building was unsuitable. During the 1914–18 war he served in the Intelligence department of the War Office, and, after the war, having been divorced from his first wife, married a wealthy American woman and practically abandoned the theatre. He tried to become a country squire in Devonshire; but as he could neither hunt, shoot, nor fish, the attempt was not successful; so he moved to Paris, and became instead a sort of professor, lecturing at universities and before learned societies on Shakespeare, the drama, and cognate themes, and writing a series of prefaces to Shakespeare's works which are full of excellent advice to producers but leave one with the impression that Shakespeare had written his plays rather as a conjurer produces rabbits from a hat, or, to put it in another way, that the thoughts and emotions expressed in the dramas had little relation to the personal life of the dramatist. In short Barker had become donnish and respectable.

Scene from Granville-Barker's production of *Twelfth Night* (1912)
with Henry Ainley as Malvolio (left) ; Hayden Coffin as Feste ;
Evelyn Millard as Olivia

Scene from Granville-Barker's production of *A Midsummer Night's Dream* (1914)
with Leon Quartermaine and Arthur Whitby

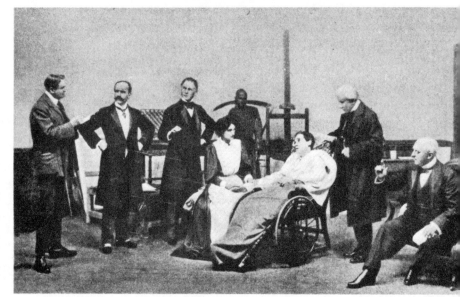

The Death Scene from Bernard Shaw's *The Doctor's Dilemma* (1906)
(left to right)—Trevor Lowe as Reporter; James Hearn as Cutler Walpol
Ben Webster as Sir Colenso Ridgeon; Lillah McCarthy as Jennifer; Granvil
Barker as Dubedat; William Farren, Jr., as Sir Patrick Cullen; Eric Lewis
Sir Ralph Bloomfield Bonnington

Louis Calvert as Undershaft and Granville-Barker as Cusins
in Shaw's *Major Barbara* (1905)

Shaw made a last-minute effort to save him from this fate. In May 1925 there was a meeting at King's College in the Strand, to hear Barker give an address. Earl Balfour was in the chair; and Forbes-Robertson moved the vote of thanks, with Shaw seconding. Shaw described to me what happened: 'When I rose the devil entered into me. I was at the top of my form. I praised Barker's speech to the skies and said that his retirement from the stage to become a professor was inexcusable. Barker as a professor! I exclaimed. It was unthinkable. Why, the speech he had just given contained enough matter to make twenty professors! I brought down the house by protesting that his retirement from active work in the theatre was a public scandal. No answer seemed possible for Barker; but Balfour tactfully saved his face by bringing the meeting to a close. Mrs Granville-Barker never forgave me for this exploit.'

The rest of Barker's life was busily academic, except for some translations from the Spanish, Mrs Barker's previous marriage having been to the millionaire founder of a great Spanish museum. Barker also wrote a play or two, which Shaw tried in vain to induce Sir Barry Jackson to produce, became an 'authority' on Shakespeare, received a few degrees, and during the 1939–45 war was a visiting professor at Yale and Harvard universities. But nearly thirty years of comfortable living, without care and without incentive, produced a man who would scarcely have been recognised by the actors who remembered their great producer. Revivals of the plays he wrote during his partnership with Shaw, *The Voysey Inheritance*, *The Madras House*, and (the now unbanned) *Waste*, have justified Shaw's encouragement of him as a playwright before, as G. B. S., quoting Swinburne, wrote in his obituary letter to *The Times Literary Supplement*, 'marriage and death and division made barren our lives'.

INDEX